Healing Your Traumatized Child

A Parent's Guide to Children's Natural Recovery Processes

Aletha J. Solter, PH.D.

SHINING STAR PRESS ★ GOLETA, CALIFORNIA

Published by Shining Star Press
Post Office Box 206
Goleta, California 93116, U.S.A.
Phone & Fax: (805) 968–1868
Email: info@awareparenting.com
Website: www.awareparenting.com (The Aware Parenting Institute)

Book design: Studio E Books, Santa Barbara

Cover photo: iStock.com/Tom Merton

Second printing 2024

PUBLISHER'S CATALOGING INFORMATION
Solter, Aletha Jauch, 1945-
Healing your traumatized child: a parent's guide to children's natural recovery processes / Aletha J. Solter
Includes bibliographical references.
ISBN: 979-8-9865429-0-4
1. Child psychology. 2. Child rearing. 3. Parenting. 4. Psychic trauma in children. I. Title.
Dewey Decimal Classification: 649.1
Library of Congress Control Number: 2022912786

Praise for *Healing Your Traumatized Child*

"As with all of Aletha Solter's books, *Healing Your Traumatized Child* is a profoundly clear and concise book with an incredibly deep understanding of children and how they heal. Dr. Solter describes exactly what happens when a child experiences trauma and precisely what parents can do to support their children's innate healing response. This is a book for every parent, because children experience trauma so much more easily than we are often led to believe. Including case studies with children who have experienced parental divorce, a traumatic dentist visit, and a wildfire evacuation, *Healing Your Traumatized Child* reassures parents about how important and powerful they are in helping their children to heal. I recommend this book so very highly."

—Marion Rose, Ph.D., author of several books, including *The Emotional Life of Babies;* Level 2 Aware Parenting instructor and regional coordinator for Aware Parenting in Australia, New Zealand, and Indonesia.

"I learned so much from this book. It is full of wisdom and clarity to help parents understand what trauma is, how we can reduce our children's exposure to trauma, and what we can do to support them when they do have traumatic experiences. It describes in depth how to create the emotional safety necessary to support our children to use their innate, natural mechanisms to release and heal from stress and trauma and return to balance. It is an inspiring exploration of the power of connection, play, laughter, and loving listening to our children's feelings to help them transform and heal. I highly recommend this book for all parents."

—Joss Goulden, Level 2 Aware Parenting instructor in Australia

"This helpful guide gives parents a clear, safe, and playful path to help children reconnect with parts of themselves lost because of trauma. Professionals working with traumatized children can use this guide as a healing bridge from their therapy office to children's homes."

—Lynn Stadler, Marriage Family Therapist in Santa Barbara, California; Founding Member of the Violet Solomon Oaklander Foundation

ALSO BY ALETHA J. SOLTER, PH.D.

The Aware Baby
Tears and Tantrums
Raising Drug-Free Kids
Attachment Play
Cooperative and Connected

This book is dedicated to all the traumatized children in the world in the hope that they will receive the support they need in order to heal.

Acknowledgments

I would like to express my deep appreciation to the following people who read the manuscript and gave me constructive feedback: my husband, Ken Solter, my daughter, Sarah Solter, and my colleague, Heather Stevenson. I am also grateful to the parents from many countries who generously shared their experiences of helping their children heal from trauma. Finally, I would like to acknowledge the pioneers who have studied childhood trauma and laid the foundation for the information in this book.

Contents

List of Charts

Warning/Disclaimer

As an educational resource for parents, this book offers information about identifying symptoms of trauma in children and recognizing their attempts to recover. It also offers suggestions for facilitating their natural healing mechanisms. These suggestions may not be appropriate for children suffering from certain physical, emotional, or behavioral problems. This book is not intended to replace psychotherapy or medical help from competent professionals. If your child is suffering from physical, emotional, or behavioral problems, it is recommended that you obtain professional advice and treatment.

The mention of specific therapies in this book is for informational purposes only and does not entail endorsement by the author. Some forms of therapy can be dangerous if carried out by improperly trained practitioners, and some therapies can cause symptoms to worsen. If you are considering choosing a therapist for yourself or your child, it is important to carefully review the therapist's credentials and references. Some traumas can overwhelm children and families, and the suggestions in this book may be inappropriate or insufficient to help children recover, especially in cases of physical or sexual abuse, neglect, medical trauma, the death of a family member, natural disasters, and terrorism or war.

The author and publisher offer no guarantee for the effectiveness of the suggestions in this book, and they shall have neither liability nor responsibility to any person or entity with respect to any damage caused, or alleged to be caused, directly or indirectly by the information contained in this book.

Healing Your Traumatized Child

Introduction

My personal experience with trauma

When I was five years old, a strange man entered my bedroom, wrapped me in a white sheet, and carried me out of my home into a waiting ambulance. I needed to be hospitalized because of an infectious illness, and no visitors were allowed during my nine-day hospital stay. I remember this experience with vivid detail. The nurses who brought me food and medicine were my only sources of social interaction, and most of the time I was left alone. I didn't experience much physical pain or discomfort, only pervasive feelings of anxiety, loneliness, boredom, and abandonment. I had picture books and craft activities, but I had nobody to talk to or play with. One evening, a friendly nurse told me a bedtime story about a sheep, and this stands out in my memory as a rare moment of connection.

While riding home from the hospital in the car with my family, my curious eight-year-old brother kept asking me questions about the hospital, but I refused to answer him. In fact, I remained mute for the rest of the day. I remember feeling totally disconnected from my family, almost as if they were strangers. By the following morning, I appeared to have returned to my usual self. However, I suffered from later posttraumatic symptoms.

This separation trauma had a major impact on me. During my entire childhood, I had a recurring nightmare of trying to use a telephone to call for help, but the telephone never worked properly, and I couldn't reach anybody. This dream always left me feeling powerless and abandoned. At the age of ten, I had chronic anxiety that my mother was going to die. This fear was triggered by the fact that she had recently begun studying for a master's degree, and her university class schedule prevented her from welcoming me home every day when I returned from school. My two older siblings were home, so I was not alone, but I missed my mother. Whenever she arrived a few minutes later than she had promised, I was convinced that she had been killed in a car accident. (My mother lived a long and healthy life well into her nineties!) Later, when I fell in love with my future husband, I felt frightened that he was going to die, and I had nightmares of being separated from him. Another impact of this experience was a fear of hospitals. I felt terrified whenever I needed to be in a hospital because of illness or surgery.

My parents were loving and attentive, but they didn't know how to help me heal from this trauma. In fact, nobody suspected at that time that such an experience could be traumatic for a child. If my parents had implemented the information in this book, I would probably not have suffered from nightmares, separation anxiety, or hospital phobia later on. Luckily, I was able to heal from this early traumatic separation through therapy as an adult, and I no longer suffer from the effects of this experience.

This hospital experience at five years of age sparked my interest in childhood trauma. As an adult, I felt motivated to help parents become aware of the impact of trauma and learn ways to support their children's healing process.

Scope of the book

The purpose of this book is to describe the impact of trauma on children and to help parents recognize and facilitate children's natural healing mechanisms. Childhood trauma can have lifelong consequences. It is now recognized as a major contributor to adult depression, anxiety, substance abuse, violence, mental illness, and even some physical illnesses. The behavioral and emotional effects of trauma often become evident early on. Aggressive, uncooperative, anxious, hyperactive, or inattentive behavior in children can be an indication of unhealed trauma. In fact, trauma-informed psychiatrists now consider childhood trauma such as abuse or neglect to be a major contributor to childhood psychiatric diagnoses.

Children are born with the ability to heal from the effects of traumatic experiences. They know how to recover and will do so spontaneously, but only if certain conditions are met. The basic requirement for healing is connection with a loving, trusted adult who helps them feel safe and who allows them to do what their bodies are biologically designed to do. Loving parents are uniquely qualified to help their children heal from trauma because parents are usually their children's primary attachment figures.

I have developed a trauma-informed approach to parenting (Aware Parenting), which is both preventive and reparative. It includes information for preventing trauma and also for helping children recover from trauma if it should occur. Three basic aspects summarize the Aware Parenting approach: how to meet children's attachment needs, how to solve behavior problems without the use of punishments or rewards (non-punitive discipline), and how to help children heal from stress and trauma. My other books cover these three aspects and offer much practical advice. The purpose of this book is to give parents practical tips for helping their children recover from trauma and also to explain more about the theory underlying the Aware Parenting approach to emotional healing. It is not necessary to read my other books in order to benefit from this one. However, if you want more practical advice for implementing all three aspects of the Aware Parenting approach, you will find answers in my other books.

This book focuses on the ways in which children (from birth to age twelve) can heal from specific traumatic events in the context of everyday life with their own parents acting as guides through the healing process. These traumas can range from a bee sting to a sudden death in the family. However, this book is not meant to replace medical advice or professional therapy. Children who have disturbing symptoms or have experienced complex trauma such as ongoing sexual or physical abuse, neglect, or domestic violence may need help that is beyond the scope of this book.

Even with loving and attentive parents, children can experience frightening or painful events, such as accidents or playground bullying, which leave them feeling traumatized and vulnerable. If your child has been traumatized, this book will help you recognize and facilitate your child's natural healing mechanisms. When children have been hurt or frightened, their behavior will indicate whether or not they have been traumatized and need support in order to recover. Unfortunately, children's symptoms of trauma and their attempts to heal are often misunderstood or considered misbehavior. You may have been led to believe that some of your child's posttraumatic behaviors or recovery efforts should be discouraged, ignored, or even punished. However, with information and support, you can learn to identify and understand your children's symptoms and behavior and effectively help them heal from trauma.

In the past, parents were advised to avoid talking about traumatic events with children because of a mistaken belief that children would forget about them if they were never mentioned. The assumption was that children would recover on their own with time, and there was very little understanding of children's need for emotional support. For example, adults told children, "Don't cry. Your mother has gone to heaven," and expected them to adapt to the tragedy of their mother's death. Physical injuries usually heal on their own with time. Unfortunately, however, time alone does not heal the emotional wounds caused by trauma. Children are born knowing how to recover, but they need support and help in order to do so.

The healing processes described in this book differ considerably from encouraging children to forget about traumatic events or to simply calm down. Healing from trauma is an active process. It involves gradually assimilating and integrating the experience by processing the emotions and completing the survival behaviors that were blocked or ineffective during the event. In this way, children can decrease the emotional charge associated with their memories of traumatic events. Traumatic experiences will always remain a part of a child's life story, but it's possible for children to release the tension in their bodies and transform their memories so that the experiences don't lead to lifelong posttraumatic symptoms.

If the traumatic event has affected you as well (such as a death in the family), you will need all the support you can find. Even if the trauma has not impacted you directly, it's only natural to feel worried, upset, helpless, guilty, or angry when your child has been traumatized and is struggling to cope. If you suffer from your own unhealed trauma or from depression, anxiety, or illness, you may find it especially difficult to implement the suggestions in this book. Stress from financial problems, relationship difficulties, or social isolation can further limit your confidence and effectiveness. Please be gentle with yourself and look for sources of support as your family strives for emotional health. Don't hesitate to seek professional therapy for yourself or your children, and remember that healing takes time.

Chapter 1

The Recognition of Childhood Trauma

IN THIS CHAPTER, I offer some background information that places childhood trauma in the context of child development, cultural history, and evolution. These three perspectives contribute to our understanding of childhood trauma and its treatment.

Children are not miniature adults

As a developmental psychologist, I am acutely aware of the differences between children and adults, and these differences affect how trauma impacts children and how they heal. An understanding of child development can help to clarify these differences.

The impact of trauma on children compared to adults

Several developmental factors help to explain why trauma affects children differently than adults. First of all, children have immature brains. From conception through the first few years after birth, the brain develops rapidly, and it continues to mature until we are at least twenty years old. Researchers have learned that the nervous system develops and organizes itself in response to experiences. One of its functions is to learn about the threat level of the environment and develop neural structures and functions that will help the child survive in that environment. If a child grows in an environment full of unpredictable threats or repeated painful, frightening experiences, that child's neurological development will be different than that of a child whose early environment is less stressful.

Early experiences can even determine which genes will express themselves, and children can be affected by stress or trauma before birth. Studies have found that maternal stress, anxiety, or depression during pregnancy can affect the fetus' developing brain. It's true that traumatic events that occur during adulthood can deeply affect a person's behavior and emotions. However, they won't impact the basic structure and function of the adult brain because it is already fully mature.

Secondly, children are more vulnerable than adults because of their total dependency on others to provide food, shelter, clothing, protection, information, connection, and love. Children don't have much power or freedom to make major decisions about their lives. As adults, we can take steps to meet our own needs and ask for help if necessary. We also have more control over our lives as well as more knowledge and resources which enable us to avoid painful or threatening situations and protect or defend ourselves when possible.

Thirdly, children have less information, experience, and perspective than adults. A two-year-old child who has surgery cannot fully understand the reason for it and has no way of knowing if the separation from her parents or her post-surgical pain will ever end. As adults, we understand the need for medical interventions, and we know that the pain won't last forever. When a young child's mother dies, he learns that major attachment figures can disappear. Abandonment becomes an entrenched part of his mindset and subconscious expectation, because he lacks the perspective to know that it doesn't always happen. When a 50-year-old man's mother dies, he will feel sad and need to grieve, but the death probably won't affect his expectation for attachment relationships.

In summary, a major difference between children and adults is that trauma during childhood provides the organizing framework for the developing brain, both neurologically and cognitively. Trauma that occurs during adulthood has behavioral, physiological, and emotional effects, but it doesn't affect neurological or cognitive development.

Healing processes in children compared to adults

The basic principles for healing from trauma are the same at all ages. However, the healing process can manifest itself quite differently in children than in adults. Most adults have decades of accumulated stress, unhealed trauma, and emotional suppression, so trauma that occurs during adulthood usually adds an additional layer to an already overloaded nervous system. Because of this fact, adults may need to proceed gradually in therapy. Young children, however, haven't lived long enough to accumulate multiple layers of unhealed trauma, so a new trauma during childhood doesn't usually trigger past unhealed traumas. This makes it possible for children to heal from specific traumas in a shorter period of time compared to adults.

We don't know to what extent children's developing nervous system becomes reprogrammed while healing from trauma. However, behavioral and neurophysiological observations indicate that the brain is extremely malleable during childhood and continually reorganizes itself during development as children acquire new experiences. Healing from early trauma while still a child can set the brain on a new developmental path.

In addition to the need for adults to proceed gradually in therapy, interventions for adults usually consist of special therapy sessions separate from everyday activities. Children, too, can benefit from therapy sessions with trained professionals. However, they can also recover from trauma in the context of daily life with loving parents. Adults don't usually have opportunities to heal in the context of everyday life because we are busy earning a living and raising children.

Another difference is that much healing can occur through children's play, an activity that comes naturally to them because of their developmental stage. As adults, we don't normally play in these ways to process our experiences. This fact can cause us to overlook or misinterpret some of children's attempts to heal.

A basic assumption of this book is that children naturally strive for emotional health, know how to heal, and will do so spontaneously when they feel safe. Children continually look for opportunities to heal from trauma, and parents can play an important role by recognizing and encouraging their attempts to do so.

Pioneers in childhood trauma

The world has been slow to recognize childhood trauma. I am grateful to researchers and practitioners from a variety of fields who have contributed to our awareness of childhood trauma, sometimes in spite of strong opposition. The ground-breaking work of these pioneers has helped shape the approach described in this book. These people fall into three categories: psychoanalytic practitioners, behavioral psychologists, and researchers in the physiology of trauma. The following sections provide a brief historical overview of these three fields.

Psychoanalytic practitioners

At the end of the 19th century, two French neurologists, Jean Martin Charcot and Pierre Janet, studied the traumatic origins of emotional distress. Sigmund Freud, a young physician from Vienna, did some clinical rotations in Paris with these neurologists and was greatly influenced by their work. After returning to Vienna, Freud further developed a trauma theory and presented a paper entitled "The Aetiology of Hysteria" to the Vienna Society for Psychiatry and Neurology in 1896. In that presentation, he mentioned several patients who appeared to have memories of early childhood sexual abuse. He proposed that the sexual abuse of young children was widespread and that it could lead to later psychological problems. This theory became known as Freud's seduction theory.

Unfortunately, Freud's colleagues were reluctant to accept the reality of childhood sexual abuse, and Freud himself had doubts about it. He later renounced his seduction theory and replaced it with his drive theory, which became the foundation of psychoanalysis. Freud based his revised theory on the assumption that most psychological problems arise not from actual trauma but from inner conflicts and desires. He claimed that his patients' reports of childhood sexual abuse reflected desires and fantasies rather than memories of actual events. This theory met with more support from his colleagues than had his original seduction theory, and the psychoanalytic approach he subsequently developed did not place much emphasis on childhood trauma.

Although Freud abandoned his original seduction theory, some of his followers did not ignore the impact of early trauma. In 1924, one of Freud's followers and collaborators, Otto Rank, wrote an influential book called *The Trauma of Birth*, in which he described birth as a child's first shock of separation. However, Freud turned against Rank for focusing on trauma, experiences, relationships, and emotions. Nevertheless, Rank's ideas influenced many therapists (both Freudian and non-Freudian) and also laid the foundation for the field of pre- and perinatal psychology (developed in the 1980s by Thomas Verny). A Hungarian follower of Freud, Sandor Ferenczi, believed in the truthfulness of his patients' reports of childhood sexual abuse and developed a trauma theory to account for adult psychological problems. Not surprisingly, this theory also led to disputes with Freud.

Several psychoanalysts in Europe have focused on the effects of maternal separation or loss. In 1940s and 1950s, René Spitz studied maternal deprivation in infants. He published several papers on this topic and also made documentary films about children in orphanages. In the 1950s and 1960s, John Bowlby, a British doctor and psychoanalyst, made a major contribution to the field of childhood trauma, culminating with his landmark, three-volume work on attachment and loss. He coined the term "attachment" to refer to a child's bond with the mother and claimed that separations from the mother during childhood could lead to dire consequences for the child. Bowlby is now recognized as the founder of attachment theory.

In the 1980s, the Swiss psychoanalyst, Alice Miller, began writing books about parental child abuse. She researched the childhoods of Adolf Hitler and other deeply disturbed people and made a clear connection between early abuse and later dysfunctional or psychopathic behavior. She abhorred the cultural injunction to honor one's parents, even if they had been abusive, and claimed that such an attitude presented a major obstacle for adults trying to heal from childhood trauma. Miller eventually broke away from traditional Freudian psychoanalytic theory because of its failure to fully acknowledge childhood abuse.

Psychoanalytically-trained practitioners in the U.S. have further contributed to the field by studying and treating child trauma victims. Beginning in the 1950s, Selma Fraiberg studied psychological trauma during infancy and early childhood and launched the field of infant mental health. Her work focused on the dysfunctional mother/child relationships involved in child abuse or neglect. Beginning in the 1980s, Lenore Terr treated many traumatized children and became well-known for her in-depth study of the posttraumatic symptoms of 26 children who had been kidnapped from a school bus in California. More recently, a psychoanalytically-trained psychiatrist, Theodore Gaensbauer, has published several case histories of infants and very young children who were traumatized by a variety of frightening events, including accidents and hospitalization.

Even though several psychoanalytically-trained practitioners have worked with, and written about, traumatized children, those who have worked with adults have focused more on their patients' inner conflicts and desires than on real-life events that may have occurred. This traditional psychoanalytic approach influenced the field of psychiatry during much of the twentieth century.

Behavioral psychologists

While some psychoanalysts were learning how to treat childhood trauma victims, behavioral psychologists were contributing to the field in a different way. In 1903, a Russian physiologist, Pavlov, first presented his discovery about conditioned reflexes in dogs. His groundbreaking work in classical conditioning established the foundation for our understanding of conditioned fear responses (and earned him a Nobel prize in medicine).

Inspired by Pavlov's work, John Watson, an American behavioral psychologist, induced conditioned fear responses in an eleven-month-old child called "little Albert" in 1920. Watson began by letting the child play with a gentle white rat, and the child initially showed no signs of fear or avoidance. Then Watson frightened the child with a loud noise each time he touched the rat. The child soon began to show fear of the rat and to avoid touching it. Later, Watson observed that the child's fear of the rat generalized to other furry objects, including a rabbit, a furry dog, a seal-skin coat, and a Santa Claus mask. These objects had not previously frightened the child.

This experiment provided the first scientific evidence that children can acquire fears through the process of classical conditioning and generalization. It inspired many other researchers (although the original study would now be considered unethical). The factors that cause a fear response by association are called conditioned stimuli. In trauma research, they are usually referred to as trauma triggers.

Classical conditioning is a form of learning. Based on the finding that fear can be a learned response, behavioral psychologists suggested that it could also be *unlearned*. In the 1950s a South African psychiatrist, Joseph Wolpe, developed an approach called systematic desensitization as a treatment for phobias. His approach was based on the idea that repeated exposures to aspects of the feared item (or event) can eventually lead to a decrease in the fear response. Later, other forms of exposure therapy were developed for adults as well as children, and some form of exposure to trauma triggers is now an integral aspect of most successful therapeutic approaches for trauma victims. Many therapists now use the term "revisiting" trauma.

(Note: The field of behaviorism includes the study of both classical conditioning and operant conditioning. Conditioned fear responses, based on research in classical conditioning, are highly relevant for understanding the approach described in this book. Operant conditioning, on the other hand, studies the use of punishments and rewards to change voluntary behaviors and is the foundation for behavior modification techniques. The Aware Parenting approach is not based on behavior modification and rejects the use of both punishments and rewards to change children's behavior.)

Researchers in the physiology of trauma

Researchers began to study the effects of stress and trauma on the brain and body in the first half of the twentieth century. In 1932, Walter Cannon, a U.S. physiologist, studied the body's response to stressful events and coined the terms "flight or fight" and "homeostasis." He recognized the role of the sympathetic nervous system in activating the body during stress or trauma. In the 1940s, a Hungarian/Canadian physiologist, Hans Selye, also studied this topic and used the engineering term "stress" in a physiological sense. He was also the first to recognize the role of glucocorticoid hormones (such as cortisol) in the stress response.

In spite of these early studies on the physiological effects of stress and trauma, the field of psychiatry as a whole has been slow to recognize childhood trauma or even adult-onset trauma. As mentioned previously, the traditional psychoanalytic tendency to ignore early trauma dominated the field during much of the twentieth century. In addition, the practice of psychiatry in the United States originated from a medical model with a search for the possible genetic causes of mental illnesses and the use of psychiatric medications to change people's moods or behavior. Because of these two influences, traditional psychiatric training did not include much information about the impact of childhood trauma. Practitioners and researchers practically ignored childhood trauma until the 1980s.

The gradual recognition of trauma occurred primarily because of combat veterans who returned from wars with a variety of serious emotional problems. After World War I, psychiatrists coined the term "shell shock" to describe their symptoms and later changed the term to "traumatic neurosis." (Neurosis is a Freudian concept and term.) After World War II and the Vietnam War, additional traumatized combat veterans sought help for emotional problems. However, many psychoanalytically-trained psychiatrists resisted the idea that trauma alone could cause psychiatric symptoms, and some thought that combat veterans who suffered from these symptoms had already been weak or "neurotic" before their war experiences. Furthermore, this new awareness of trauma did not extend to childhood trauma.

In 1980, the American Psychiatric Association finally recognized the potential impact of trauma, rejecting the Freudian term neurosis and coining the diagnostic term "Post-Traumatic Stress Disorder" (PTSD) in the third edition of their *Diagnostic and Statistical Manual of Mental Disorders (DSM-3)*. PTSD was included in their category of anxiety disorders. Later, the organization Zero to Three conceived of a trauma-related diagnosis specifically for young children (originally called Traumatic Stress Disorder), which they included in their publication entitled *Diagnostic Classification of Mental Health and Developmental Disorders of Infancy and Early Childhood* (published in 1994).

Following the creation of the term PTSD, the women's movement began to raise awareness of childhood sexual abuse as a possible cause of PTSD. Almost a century after Freud had first proposed a sexual abuse theory of mental disturbances (Freud's seduction theory), professionals and the general public finally began to accept the prevalence and devastating impact of childhood sexual abuse.

The new diagnostic term PTSD inspired research in the neurobiology of trauma as well as increased recognition of the impact of childhood trauma. The development of sophisticated brain imaging techniques and the discovery of neurotransmitters has made it possible for researchers to study the impact of traumatic experiences on the brain. Bessel van der Kolk, a Dutch/American psychiatrist and one of the main pioneers in this field, has published numerous articles and books on this topic. Another psychiatrist and trauma researcher, Bruce Perry, has also contributed to the field by describing how temporary adaptive responses to trauma (physiological states of hyperarousal or dissociation) can become chronic traits.

By 2009, Bessel van der Kolk had accumulated extensive evidence indicating that children suffering from psychiatric disorders have usually experienced early trauma, such as abuse or neglect, and that these experiences have affected their brain. He noticed that the diagnostic criteria for PTSD didn't always fit these traumatized children, who often received other kinds of psychiatric diagnoses (such as attention deficit hyperactivity disorder or oppositional defiant disorder). However, those diagnoses didn't locate the root cause of these children's problems, which was often early trauma. Based on four years of research with colleagues, he drafted a proposal for a new diagnostic term, Developmental Trauma Disorder (DTD), which he hoped would replace or incorporate many of the childhood diagnoses currently being used.

Just as with Freud's original trauma theory, however, van der Kolk's emphasis on childhood trauma met with strong resistance. Unfortunately, the American Psychiatric Association rejected his proposed new diagnostic term (Developmental Trauma Disorder) and did not include it in the fifth edition of the *Diagnostic and Statistical Manual of Mental Disorders (DSM-5)*, published in 2013.

Additional information about the impact of childhood trauma came from the now-famous study of adverse childhood experiences (ACE), published in 1998. This was the first large-scale study to look at the relationship between various forms of child adversity and later health outcomes. The researchers identified seven categories of adverse experiences, including various forms of abuse and neglect as well as household dysfunction (such as parental substance abuse). The results indicated a strong correlation between the number of adverse childhood experiences and negative health outcomes in adults, including substance abuse, depression, obesity, heart disease, cancer, lung disease, skeletal fractures, and liver disease. Based on this study, the World Health Organization developed a questionnaire of adverse childhood experiences, which indicates recognition of the impact of childhood trauma.

Awareness of childhood trauma increasingly informs and influences therapeutic practices and research. In addition to the pioneers mentioned in this section, innovative therapists outside of these fields have built on these foundations and further contributed to our understanding and treatment of childhood trauma.

Human vulnerability to trauma

Human infancy is characterized by an immature brain and a long period of helplessness and dependency, which makes infants highly vulnerable to trauma. They are easily startled, confused, and traumatized by frightening events, physical pain, sudden changes, loud noises, separation from their parents, and unmet needs. In order to survive and thrive, they must rely on their parents' ability to meet their needs for protection, warmth, nourishment, and emotional support.

When parents are suffering from their own unhealed childhood trauma, their parenting behavior will be less than optimal, and they could inadvertently cause their vulnerable infants to suffer by failing to protect them or meet their needs. If you struggle to be the kind of parent you want to be, one reason could be that you are still suffering from the effects of your own early traumas that occurred when you yourself were powerless and vulnerable.

Evolutionary biologists have proposed several theories to explain the long infancy of our species. One theory suggests that our bipedalism (walking on two feet) would limit the width of the female pelvis for structural reasons, resulting in the need for the fetus to be born before the head grows any larger. A related theory asserts that the pelvic width is also limited by the need to support a heavy fetus during pregnancy while the mother stands or walks. Because of natural selection, infants with a smaller head circumference at birth (and therefore with a less developed brain) would have been more likely to survive the birth process. Those with a larger head would have caused obstructed labor. Other biologists have emphasized the metabolic constraints on the mother required to carry an infant with a larger brain to term. Yet another theory suggests that a long infancy and childhood is advantageous for our species because it allows time for the transmission of language and other cultural knowledge.

Whatever the evolutionary explanation for our long infancy, our early vulnerability provides a possible explanation for the high prevalence of childhood trauma in human beings, which makes our species prone to trauma-induced mental disturbances. We can counteract this human susceptibility by helping adults heal from childhood trauma and, even more importantly, by helping children recover while they are still young.

Chapter 2

The Neurobiology of Trauma

I DEFINE A TRAUMATIC EVENT as anything that causes physical or emotional pain or that threatens a child's wellbeing. Traumas can be minor events, such as the loss of a toy or a bee sting, or major life-changing events such as the death of a parent or a terrorist attack. Anything that the child interprets as threatening can be traumatic, even when it does not pose a real danger. A person wearing a wolf mask could terrify a young child even though there is no real threat. Children can also be traumatized by adults' reactions of terror, because our brains are wired to be acutely aware of fear signals that other people display through movements, postures, facial expressions, and verbalizations.

Children differ in their reactions to frightening events. Something could traumatize one child but not another. Their interpretation of experiences depends on many factors, including their developmental stage, innate temperament, previous trauma history, state of health, and the presence or absence of attachment figures.

Interpersonal trauma can occur when a child's primary attachment figures (usually the parents) inflict harm on the child. Unfortunately, child abuse and neglect occur worldwide because of the parents' own trauma history combined with lack of resources or support for parents. Interpersonal trauma typically causes more pervasive posttraumatic symptoms in children than trauma caused by people outside the family or by external events and is also more difficult to heal.

Before we can help children heal from trauma, we need to understand exactly how traumatic experiences affect them. Human beings, like many other animals, have two primary reactions to threats, which evolved to enhance our survival. One reaction is to become active in order to defend ourselves or escape from the dangerous situation. This is called the hyperarousal response, also known as fight or flight. The other survival reaction is dissociation, also known as the freeze response. Both hyperarousal and dissociation can occur on a continuum ranging from mild to extreme. These two strategies correspond to physiological states controlled by the autonomic nervous system, which, in turn, is controlled by several other brain regions by means of hormones and neurotransmitters.

Hyperarousal during trauma (the fight/flight response)

When children feel threatened, they often react by actively attempting to defend themselves or escape. This fight or flight response represents a highly effective survival mechanism. If a five-year-old girl has an older brother who enjoys overpowering and tickling her, she will probably use self-defense behaviors to yell, hit, kick, scratch, or bite her brother until he lets her go. That would be the fight response. For the flight response, imagine a two-year-old child going for a walk with his mother. Feeling confident and independent, he walks a short distance ahead of her until a dog behind a fence suddenly startles him by barking loudly. He screams in terror and runs back to his mother as fast as he can until he reaches the safety of her arms. In this situation, the child uses flight as a way to escape from the perceived threat.

After the terrorist attacks in New York City on September 11, 2001, researchers interviewed parents of young children about their reactions and behaviors during and immediately after the attacks as the day unfolded. Many parents described hyperarousal and panic-like behaviors. One mother said that her 14-month-old boy started screaming and kicking when she tried to put him into his stroller so they could evacuate from their apartment. Another reported that her two-and-a-half-year-old son covered his ears while yelling repeatedly, "It's too loud, it's too loud" during the collapse of the second tower. A three-year-old girl started screaming, "Where's Daddy? Where's Daddy?" Many parents described unusually high levels of distractibility, agitation, and motor activity, such as running around uncontrollably.

In addition to yelling or screaming, body movements are important aspects of both fight and flight. Children actively use their bodies whenever possible to defend themselves or escape from a threatening situation, even if all they can do is kick their legs, run around, or cover their ears. Two physiological systems play a role in facilitating these body movements: the sympathetic nervous system and the hypothalamic-pituitary-adrenal (HPA) system. The brain controls both of these systems and immediately activates them during a threatening event.

As explained in Chapter 1, Walter Cannon first described the fight or flight response in 1932. The sympathetic nervous system increases the child's heart rate and blood flow to the arms and legs. The main chemicals involved are catecholamines (adrenaline and noradrenaline). At the same time, less blood goes to the intestines because digestion would be a waste of precious energy needed for immediate survival.

The primary function of the HPA system is to increase the amount of sugar in the blood so the child has immediate energy resources for fight or flight. The HPA system functions mostly via hormones, beginning in the hypothalamus, which stimulates the pituitary gland to produce adrenocorticotropic hormone (ACTH). This hormone stimulates the adrenal cortex to release glucocorticoid hormones, which help to increase blood sugar levels. One of these glucocorticoid hormones (cortisol) can be measured in blood or saliva samples and used as an indication of stress levels.

In summary, the hyperarousal response facilitates active movements by sending the blood to the arms and legs, where it is most needed for self-defense or escape, and by ensuring that enough energy resources are immediately available. These processes all occur automatically when a child feels threatened.

Dissociation during trauma (the freeze response)

When children are unable to defend themselves or escape from a dangerous situation, they automatically use another survival strategy called dissociation. They become quiet, still, and numb. Some people use the terms shutdown, freeze, surrender, immobility, or shock to describe this response. Like the hyperarousal response, dissociation has adaptive survival value. The immobility helps children conserve energy, and the numbness helps them cope with emotional or physical pain.

In the late 1800s, the French neurologist, Pierre Janet (mentioned in Chapter 1), was the first person to use the term dissociation to refer to the tendency to shut down and become immobile during traumatic experiences. He described dissociation as a splitting off from normal consciousness and voluntary control. Although Freud did not emphasize early trauma, he also referred to dissociative states, which he described as altered and abnormal states of consciousness.

The tendency to freeze while under threat also occurs in animals, both in laboratory settings and in the wild. The Russian physiologist, Pavlov, observed similar states in animals during his experiments and used the term transmarginal inhibition. More recently, animal behavior specialists refer to this temporary immobility as tonic immobility, and it commonly occurs when an animal is unable to escape a predator. One purpose is that it serves to avoid detection by predators, thereby enhancing survival. Another function is that it conserves energy and numbs pain, so the animal (even if injured) will be able to spring into action if an opportunity for escape presents itself.

One of the first recorded cases of traumatic dissociation in a child was published in a 1942 report about the psychological effects of the London air raids during World War II. A four-year-old girl who survived an attack, but whose parents did not, remained sitting for several days in the exact spot where her mother had left her. She did not speak, eat, or play, and she had to be moved "like an automaton."

In the study mentioned previously about the effects on young children of the New York City terrorist attacks in 2001, many parents observed dissociation (rather than hyperarousal) in their children on the day of the attacks. One mother described the reunion on the street with her two-and-a-half-year-old daughter who had been evacuated from her daycare center with other children. The child had watched the airplane hit the building and was outside when the first tower collapsed. She had been caught in the debris and dust but was physically unharmed. The mother described her daughter as catatonic, dazed, and totally silent. She did not say a word to her parents when they reached her, nor did she cry. Other parents described their young children as withdrawn, quieter than usual, white as a sheet, petrified, and incredibly cooperative. Many parents also mentioned that their children slept at unusual times that day, or they slept so deeply that they could not be awakened. One child had a seizure and was taken to a hospital while his sibling slept through the whole thing.

In spite of the early discovery of trauma-induced dissociation, researchers and clinicians during most of the twentieth century focused almost exclusively on Walter Cannon's fight or flight response (hyperarousal) and tended to ignore dissociation as a possible reaction to trauma. Beginning in the 1980s, researchers and clinicians revived the concept of dissociation during trauma and now use the term to describe a continuum of behaviors ranging from daydreaming to fainting.

With growing awareness of traumatic dissociation, scientists began to study its neurobiology, which is even more complex than the neurobiology of hyperarousal and involves several parts of the nervous system. The parasympathetic nervous system (specifically the vagus nerve) becomes dominant, reducing heart rate and blood pressure. Dissociation also involves high levels of endogenous opioids (endorphins), which numb physical pain and reduce emotions of fear and anger, sometimes even producing narcotic-like euphoria. Dopamine, which plays a role in addictive behaviors, is also involved in dissociation. The high levels of both endorphins and dopamine may help to explain why dissociative states can be both pleasurable and addictive.

Interestingly, glucocorticoid levels (such as cortisol) usually remain high during dissociation and immobility, as do circulating blood levels of adrenaline. This implies that the body is still prepared for fight or flight if such a survival strategy should become necessary and possible. Dissociation therefore represents a temporary brake on an activated system, similar to driving a car with one foot on the accelerator and one on the brake. Some researchers distinguish different types of dissociation, but all agree that the dissociation continuum indicates unique physiological states which differ from either hyperarousal or a balanced state of homeostasis.

Painful medical interventions and sexual abuse are especially potent triggers for dissociation in young children. The younger the children, the greater their tendency to use dissociation instead of hyperarousal as a survival strategy because they can't easily fight or escape. There is also evidence that children are more likely to suffer later on from posttraumatic symptoms if they dissociated during the original trauma.

Trauma and memory

In order for frightening events to cause later posttraumatic symptoms, we must encode them in some kind of memory storage and retrieval system. Without any memory of threatening events, there would be no posttraumatic symptoms. This would probably make our lives more pleasant, but unfortunately, our species would have died out long ago if we lacked this kind of memory! We would not have been able to learn any survival strategies from our experiences with dangerous situations. To enhance survival, memories of trauma have evolved to be strong and persistent.

Researchers used to assume that children could not remember anything before the development of language. However, this assumption has been proven incorrect. There is evidence that young children can remember highly salient, traumatic events that occurred during infancy, when the brain systems for storing everyday memories were not yet fully developed. Studies have shown that young children can sometimes reveal memories of trauma that occurred during the first year after birth through symbolic play or even verbally. Although a child might not remember details of her day-to-day life during early infancy, highly arousing, traumatic experiences appear to be stored in a special way that makes them readily available for later recall.

Neutral (non-traumatic) memories of personal experiences are processed and stored primarily in the hippocampus, the temporal cortex, and the prefrontal cortex. These parts of the brain are not fully developed at birth. As children's brains develop, they gradually become more effective at encoding and storing memories of neutral experiences, and by two to three years of age, children have fairly good long-term memory.

Traumatic experiences, on the other hand, are processed and stored differently than neutral experiences. They are not encoded in memory as a coherent narrative with a beginning and an end but rather as a variety of painful emotions, multiple sensory impressions (touch, sight, sound, pain, etc.), body movements, and physiological states (hunger, heart rate, etc.). Studies of the neurobiology of trauma indicate that the amygdala, which is fully functional at birth, plays a major role in processing and storing the emotions associated with frightening events. This role includes conditioned fear responses and the fight or flight reaction (hyperarousal). Memories of sensory impressions, body movements, and physiological states associated with trauma are stored in other parts of the brain (including some of the same areas involved in neutral memory storage). Even when children have enough language skills to talk about a traumatic event, they find it difficult to tell a coherent story because of the complex and fragmented manner in which various aspects of these memories are stored in the brain.

Many people assume incorrectly that our memory of personal experiences functions like the digital storage system of a computer, which saves documents without modifying them. However, human memory functions differently than computers. Cognitive neuroscience informs us that our memories are highly subject to change. In fact, every time we recall a past experience, our brain actively *reconstructs* it and then stores it in a slightly modified form. This is the case for both neutral and traumatic memories. We reconstruct our personal memories by accessing the stored sensory impressions combined with the emotions that we experienced at the time. However, we also incorporate *new* experiences, sensations, emotions, and knowledge without any awareness that we are doing so, and these updated memories replace the old ones. Researchers refer to this process as memory reconsolidation.

The continual modification of memories helps to explain why siblings who grew up in the same family often have different memories of shared childhood experiences. These discrepancies can cause confusion and even arguments. However, our tendency to transform memories is very useful because it lies at the root of our ability to heal from trauma.

Sometimes children have no conscious memory of traumatic events, not even of disconnected sensory impressions or emotions. Total amnesia can occur following prolonged or repetitive levels of extreme traumatic stress. This memory retrieval failure appears to be caused by high levels of corticosteroids and endorphins in the brain and is related to dissociation. Although children may not consciously recall such overwhelming traumatic events, the experiences are nevertheless stored in many parts of the brain, and posttraumatic symptoms can occur unexpectedly later in life (sometimes even decades later).

Posttraumatic reactions

Traumatic experiences don't always result in posttraumatic symptoms. A significant determining factor is whether or not children feel protected during the event. Additionally, posttraumatic symptoms are more likely to occur when children's attempts to escape or defend themselves are ineffective, especially when they dissociate (freeze and go numb) during the trauma. Another factor is whether or not they have the opportunity to connect with a trusted adult and process their emotions in the immediate aftermath of a threatening event. When these conditions are not met, children are more likely to suffer from posttraumatic symptoms.

Trauma triggers

One indication of unhealed trauma is a strong reaction to anything that reminds children of the event. These reminders are called trauma triggers. It's important to remember that our persistent memory of traumatic events, combined with our sensitivity to trauma triggers, evolved to enhance our survival as a species, because many frightening events throughout prehistory were actual threats to our survival. If a rustling sound in the woods preceded an encounter with a predatory animal, that same sound on another day would have triggered a fight or flight reaction for our prehistoric ancestors. Modern humans have inherited a tendency to overreact to anything that even remotely resembles a previous trauma, even when there is no actual threat. In fact, all mammals and many other species have this same tendency to assess the environment and to overestimate potential threats rather than to underestimate them.

If the child's brain interprets a trauma trigger as threatening, his body will automatically enter a state of either hyperarousal or dissociation. This means that these physiological survival methods can become conditioned (learned) responses, easily activated by conditioned stimuli (trauma triggers). Nowadays, however, most frightening experiences for children are not emergency situations that threaten their survival, yet their bodies react as if this were the case. Instead of saving their lives, this overreaction to trauma triggers can become maladaptive and interfere with their lives.

A conditioned hyperarousal response can be illustrated by a five-year-old boy whose older sister frequently hits him. One day, on the playground at school, an older girl accidentally bumps into the boy during a ball game. This incident triggers a subconscious memory of his sister's aggressive behavior, and the boy's brain incorrectly interprets the accidental physical contact by a playmate as intentional aggression. He reacts by angrily hitting the girl.

Conditioned dissociation can be illustrated by a three-year-old girl who had a painful medical procedure. When her parents bring her back to the medical clinic for a later check-up, she sits quietly in the waiting room while sucking her thumb and staring into space. She shows no interest in the available toys and barely responds when her parents speak to her. In this example, the medical clinic functions as a trauma trigger, which reminds her of her painful procedure. Her brain interprets the situation as threatening even when she knows that she will not have any procedure done that day, and her body responds with dissociation.

These examples both involve external trauma triggers (the touch of another child or the medical clinic setting). Trauma triggers can be any of the basic sensory impressions that the brain has stored in memory from the original trauma, including touch, vision, sound, smell, taste, temperature, pain, and pressure. Children can also be triggered in the absence of external sensory impressions because memories of trauma can arise spontaneously in the form of mental images, flashbacks, or nightmares, as well as from internal body sensations.

When children encounter an external or internal trauma trigger without feeling safe, their body typically reacts with the same survival mechanism that they used during the original trauma. If they reacted with hyperarousal, they will tend to become hyperaroused during a later trauma trigger, and if they dissociated during the original trauma, later triggers will tend to cause dissociation. The neural circuits that control these reactions become strengthened (sensitized) each time the brain activates them, so the tendency to go into states of hyperarousal or dissociation grows stronger with each trauma trigger. Eventually, even minor trauma triggers can cause these reactions. The regular unbidden exposure to both external and internal trauma triggers can cause some traumatized children to be in a constant state of hyperarousal or dissociation during months or even years after a traumatic event has occurred. Some children spend more time in one state than the other, while others alternate between the two.

This book focuses on the impact of specific traumatic events on children. However, a major trauma may not be necessary for chronic hyperarousal or dissociation to occur. An accumulation of stress or unhealed mini-traumas can affect children's bodies in the same way as a single threatening event because their brain interprets a build-up of stress as a threat to their wellbeing. Children can accumulate stress from daily overstimulation, anxiety, disappointments, frustrations, unmet needs, criticisms, punishment, their parents' stress, or unrealistic expectations by adults. Consequently, their body prepares them for survival in the only way it knows how: to fight, flee, or freeze, even when those responses may not serve any immediate short-term function for survival.

Luckily, trauma triggers don't always cause these reactions. Like traumatic experiences themselves, trauma triggers affect children differently depending on how safe they feel. If they feel unsafe and unprotected, they are more likely to react to the trauma trigger as if the original trauma were happening again. However, if children are exposed to a trauma trigger while feeling safe, protected, and connected to a supportive person, their assessment of danger shifts. They are less likely to become hyperaroused or dissociated and more likely to use the situation for healing from the trauma, as described in the following chapters.

Symptoms of posttraumatic hyperarousal and dissociation

The following chart lists some typical behaviors that can indicate posttraumatic hyperarousal or dissociation (although some of them could have other causes). If children act in these ways when there is no immediate threat, it's possible that they are suffering from unhealed trauma and are being triggered in some way but do not feel safe enough to use the situation for healing. They could also be suffering from an accumulation of stress. The primary function of these behaviors is self-protection.

Symptoms of posttraumatic hyperarousal and dissociation in children

Posttraumatic hyperarousal (fight/flight response) *Sympathetic nervous system is dominant*	Posttraumatic dissociation (freeze/numbing response) *Parasympathetic nervous system is dominant*
The child may be hyperactive, agitated, distractible, impulsive, hypervigilant, over-reactive, easily startled, defiant, non-compliant, aggressive, or destructive.	The child may be quiet, passive, compliant, detached, inattentive, unresponsive, unemotional, obsessive, or compulsive.
The child may hit or bite other people, initiate fights, throw or break things, have difficulty sitting still or concentrating, have difficulty falling asleep, awaken frequently at night, or yell/scream in anger or terror (without tears).	The child may have self-soothing habits (thumb sucking, self-rocking), be attached to a special blanket or toy, frequently daydream, masturbate excessively, harm himself (head-banging, hair-pulling, self-cutting), or faint easily when experiencing strong emotions.

Both of these physiological states begin as automatic, involuntary reactions during trauma, and hyperarousal symptoms tend to remain involuntary. However, children can learn to dissociate voluntarily, and they do this when they don't receive the support and emotional safety that they need or when their hyperarousal behaviors lead to punishment or rejection. A typical way for children to dissociate is to suck their thumb or rock themselves back and forth.

Of much greater concern are children who purposely harm themselves (for example, by pulling their hair out or cutting themselves) in order to benefit from the release of endorphins which numb both physical and emotional pain during dissociation. As mentioned previously, dissociative states are both pleasurable and addictive, so self-harming behaviors can be considered a form of addiction. Children who intentionally harm themselves need immediate interventions. Interestingly, the use of an opiate inhibitor (naltrexone) has been effective in reducing hair-pulling in children. This drug blocks the endorphin euphoria that accompanies dissociation, thereby reducing children's motivation to harm themselves. The need for medication can be decreased or avoided by helping these children recover from the traumatic experiences that lie at the root of their need to dissociate.

This book is not a substitute for professional advice or treatment. In addition to self-harming behaviors, some of the other behaviors mentioned in this section can indicate serious emotional or medical problems. Children who faint easily could have an underlying medical condition that should be addressed, and children who are destructive or aggressive towards others obviously need help. It's important to seek professional advice whenever you feel concerned about your child's behavior or suspect a medical problem.

These behaviors indicating posttraumatic hyperarousal and dissociation do not include all of the typical symptoms of traumatized children. They often display other posttraumatic symptoms, which are not necessarily related to specific trauma triggers. These include nightmares, a loss of recently acquired skills, bedwetting, increased resistance to separation or changes in routines, eating disorders, avoidance of trauma reminders, tics, and compulsive re-enactments of trauma. Children also suffer from a variety of posttraumatic emotions which are summarized in the next chapter.

Traumatized children also often complain of physical symptoms such as headaches, stomachaches, nausea, dizziness, pain, numbness, stiffness, heart palpitations, shortness of breath, or fatigue even though there are no obvious physical causes. These very real sensations can result from the physiological changes that occur in their bodies during trauma (and later trauma triggers). It's important to take these complaints seriously and seek medical advice whenever your child has physical symptoms such as these, but it's also helpful to understand that these body sensations can be caused by trauma.

In the long term, the constant presence of stress hormones in a child's body can contribute to health problems. Chronically high levels of adrenaline can lead to high blood pressure, heart attacks, and strokes, while chronically high cortisol levels can lower their immune response, inhibit their growth, cause brain damage, and increase the likelihood of diabetes later in life. Helping children heal from trauma, therefore, not only benefits them immediately but can also prevent later stress-related illnesses.

Misinterpretations of posttraumatic reactions

Unfortunately, adults sometimes misinterpret posttraumatic behaviors when they don't recognize the connection with unhealed trauma. One incorrect assumption is that the child is misbehaving and requires some kind of disciplinary action. Hyperarousal behaviors often cause problems for parents and teachers, who feel that their only choice is to use rewards or punishments to change them. This approach to discipline may result in a temporary reduction in some of these behaviors, but I do not recommend it because it will not solve the underlying cause. Furthermore, it could add additional stress to a child who is already suffering, and it could cause a child in hyperarousal simply to switch to dissociation.

A second incorrect assumption is that symptoms of hyperarousal or dissociation reflect the child's personality or an inborn temperament trait. When these physiological states become chronic, we tend to label children accordingly. When describing your children, you might be tempted to say "he's our wild child," or "she's our calm little angel," or "he has an aggressive streak like his dad," with the assumption that your child was born that way. It's important to remember that you could be describing a physiological coping mechanism rather than your child's real personality. Many parents have told me that their children appear to change personalities after they begin to heal from trauma.

A third misinterpretation is to assume that these behaviors indicate a psychiatric disorder. Unfortunately, when parents seek help for children with these behaviors, professionals don't always consider the role of past trauma. Children with hyperarousal behaviors often receive a diagnosis relating to hyperactivity, noncompliance, or aggression. Parents are less likely to seek help for children who frequently dissociate, because they are quiet and withdrawn, and their behavior doesn't usually bother other people. However, if these children do get diagnosed, it's usually with a disorder relating to anxiety, depression, inattention, or obsessive/compulsive behavior. In both cases, parents might be led to believe that the cause is genetic and that the appropriate remedy is medication. When unhealed trauma lies at the root of these behaviors, psychiatric medication will only mask the symptoms without helping the child heal.

Misinterpretations of posttraumatic reactions

Possible misinterpretation	Correct information
Children with hyperarousal behaviors are misbehaving and need discipline.	Children with hyperarousal behaviors don't consciously choose to act in these ways.
Symptoms of hyperarousal or dissociation reflect a child's inborn temperament.	Symptoms of hyperarousal or dissociation are often temporary physiological coping mechanism.
Symptoms of hyperarousal or dissociation indicate a genetically-caused psychiatric disorder that requires medication.	Symptoms of hyperarousal or dissociation can be reactions to trauma and can disappear without medication.

The posttraumatic behaviors mentioned in this chapter occur when children do not feel completely safe and have not yet begun to heal. When children feel safe and connected after encountering a trauma trigger, they make use of the situation to activate natural biological healing processes which include laughter, specific kinds of play, crying, tantrums, and body movements. The following chapters explain how these healing mechanisms help children recover from trauma.

Chapter 3

Posttraumatic Emotions and Basic Principles of Healing

TRAUMA RESULTS WHEN children's attempts to defend themselves or escape are unsuccessful or when they give up and dissociate. They can recover in the immediate aftermath of a frightening event or at any time later on, and the healing process is the same whenever it occurs. If they don't have an opportunity to recover, they will become easily triggered by trauma reminders later on and may remain stuck in reactions of hyperarousal or dissociation.

The physiological survival reactions of hyperarousal and dissociation, described in the previous chapter, are driven by the painful emotions that arise during frightening and threatening experiences and also during later trauma triggers. These emotions function as a warning signal to the child's brain that it's necessary to take actions that will enhance self-protection and survival.

One effect of hyperarousal and dissociation is that they immediately mask or numb both physical and emotional pain. When survival is the primary concern, continued awareness of painful emotions and body sensations would be distracting and counterproductive. A girl who struggles against her brother's abusive tickling by hitting and biting him (symptoms of hyperarousal) is reacting automatically to a threat but might not be aware of the underlying terror that mobilized her defensive actions. A boy who dissociates by cowering in a corner while sucking his thumb during his father's drunken rage might not be aware of his own rage or terror. In fact, if he openly panicked or confronted his father, he would risk being beaten by him.

In order to recover, children need to complete the natural bio-logical recovery processes that normally occur after threatening events. These processes involve emergence from a state of hyper-arousal or dissociation, awareness and release of painful emotions, and actions which convince their brain that the trauma has been successfully confronted and overcome. Healing from trauma is therefore equivalent to completing something unfinished, and the result is a transformation of children's memory.

This chapter describes the various emotions that can occur during and after traumatic experiences and explains how children's awareness of these emotions can function as a gateway into the healing process under the right conditions.

Posttraumatic emotions

Terror and rage are the primary and most immediate emotions caused by trauma. Others are grief, powerlessness, guilt, and con-fusion. Each of these has a possible range of intensity from mild to intense. These emotions can linger for months or even years when children don't have opportunities to heal from trauma.

Terror

Trauma causes children to feel vulnerable and frightened. They don't know if, or when, something bad will happen again. Increased separation anxiety commonly occurs after a traumatic event. The mother of a three-year-old girl consulted with me because her daughter refused to sleep alone in a room after a thief had bro-ken into their home while they were away. In the study about the September 11th terrorist attacks in New York City, many parents reported new intense separation anxiety in their children. Eight months after the terrorist attack, a four-year-old girl still needed her mother to be within eyesight at all times.

In addition to general anxiety, a single traumatic event typically results in specific phobias acquired through the process of classical conditioning. Because of the high level of perceived threat in traumatic experiences, all it takes is a single experience to cause a conditioned fear of anything associated with the frightening event. A child who has been bitten by a dog will probably develop a dog phobia. For months after the New York City terrorist attacks, many children who lived near the World Trade Center had a fear of airplanes, loud noises, and sirens. A little girl developed a sudden new fear of the television show that she had been watching when the first plane crashed into the World Trade Center tower near her apartment.

Trauma triggers can become generalized and lead to fear and avoidance of related stimuli. A child who has survived a wildfire might develop a phobia that generalizes to matches, candles, cigarette smoke, or images of fires. Some of the children who witnessed the terrorist attacks on the World Trade Center in New York City developed a generalized fear of all tall buildings.

Rage

Children naturally feel angry at the people who hurt or frighten them. When there is no obvious perpetrator, as in the case of accidents, children often find someone or something to blame so they can have a target at which to direct their anger. A little girl who falls off a tricycle and skins her knee might feel angry at another child who was in her way, even though it wasn't his fault. She might even direct her anger at the tricycle and blame it for tipping over!

Children often express their anger as hatred or even intense rage. Their parents (often their mothers) become common targets because parents are the people whom children count on the most for protection. When children experience a distressing event, they naturally blame their parents for not preventing it, even though this might be totally illogical. A boy might scream "I hate you" to his mother simply because she wants him to wear nice clothes to his grandfather's funeral. In reality, the boy is probably feeling angry at whatever caused his grandfather's death.

Grief

Traumatic experiences often cause deep sadness, especially those involving loss. The death of a parent or other family member is a devastating experience for children. Even temporary separations from primary attachment figures can cause grief in babies and young children. A parent's illness or depression represents loss of that person's attention and availability and can cause grief and anxiety in young children, similar to separation trauma. Grief can also be caused by other kinds of losses such as the death of a pet, a broken or lost toy, a friend who moves away, or a move to a new home.

Disappointment is another form of loss. A boy who was looking forward to his grandparents' arrival in time for his birthday party will feel deeply disappointed if something prevents them from coming.

Feelings of depression and hopelessness often follow a traumatic event. Many of the children who survived a California school bus kidnapping felt that they would not live very long and that they had nothing to look forward to.

Powerlessness

Feelings of powerlessness and helplessness are major components of all traumatic experiences and can cause children to resist anything that takes away their feeling of control. Even children who haven't been traumatized often feel powerless simply because of their immaturity and dependence on others to care for them and make major decisions about their lives. Traumatic experiences always add an additional layer of powerlessness.

Powerlessness can also express itself by giving up on attempts to exert control. This feeling of resignation can cause children to feel paralyzed and unable to make decisions when they have the opportunity to do so.

Guilt and shame

Children can feel guilty when they mistakenly think that they caused a traumatic event, and this feeling is common in young children. They might feel that their uncooperative behavior caused their parents' divorce or their anger caused their grandmother's death.

Children raised with punitive methods of discipline are especially likely to blame themselves and feel guilty when a traumatic event occurs. If they have an accident or illness, they could have a misconception that they are being punished for something they did wrong.

Feelings of shame and worthlessness can occur when children experience adult anger, punishment, or abuse. Even nonviolent punishment such as loss of privileges or the use of time-out can leave children feeling guilty, ashamed, or unloved. When adults yell or hit, children assume that it must be their own fault for being imperfect in some way, and those who have been sexually abused often blame themselves. In extreme cases, guilt and shame can lead to self-hatred.

Confusion

Feelings of confusion accompany all traumatic experiences. Like adults, children strive to understand why bad things happen and can benefit from age-appropriate explanations. Even when children know the cause, however, traumatic experiences can feel overwhelming, especially if they occur unexpectedly and significantly alter their life. After a natural disaster, terrorist attack, medical emergency, or the sudden death of a family member, children are faced with too much information to assimilate and process all at once. These feelings of confusion and overstimulation can make traumatized children resist change or new experiences, and they often crave a return to normal routines.

Posttraumatic emotions

- Terror

- Rage

- Grief

- Powerlessness

- Guilt and shame

- Confusion

Basic principles of healing
Revisiting trauma

The approach described in this book is based on the assumption that healing from trauma involves the transformation of traumatic memories. The first step is to revisit the trauma in some way in order to retrieve the memories. This is the basic premise of exposure therapies (inspired by classical conditioning research), which have been used in efforts to help traumatized people. The two main traditional exposure therapy techniques are systematic desensitization and intense or prolonged exposure therapy. This book describes a process that incorporates exposure to trauma triggers but that differs from these two approaches.

Systematic desensitization is based on the principle of counter-conditioning. The goal is to pair the fear-evoking stimulus (the trauma trigger) with an emotional state that is incompatible with anxiety, such as deep relaxation or pleasure. This approach involves gradual exposure to trauma triggers in order to avoid overwhelming the client. Gradual desensitization with relaxation can be effective for some fears (such as a fear of snakes) but has not proven to be very effective in reducing posttraumatic symptoms.

Intense or prolonged exposure therapy is based on the principle of extinction of the classically conditioned fear response and uses intense exposure to trauma triggers. It leads to high levels of anxiety, which eventually decrease (become extinguished) because the feared consequences do not occur. However, there are two disadvantages of intense exposure therapy. First of all, even though fear decreases after the therapy, it can return later on during periods of stress. Secondly, prolonged or intense exposure therapies have a high risk of overwhelming traumatized people and causing re-traumatization. Some of the early intense exposure techniques for combat veterans with PTSD used war videos as trauma triggers, which produced strong emotional reactions. Some veterans benefited from these exposure therapy sessions, but others felt re-traumatized and overwhelmed, and their symptoms of hyperarousal and dissociation increased.

Therapists learned from these early intense exposure approaches that people can become overwhelmed by trauma triggers when they don't feel safe and when the triggers resemble the original trauma too closely. Many trauma-informed therapists now use a gentler, more gradual approach so people will not become overwhelmed by painful memories, emotions, body sensations, and physiological reactions. The term "revisiting" trauma has replaced the former term "reliving" trauma.

Children can revisit trauma in a variety of safe, indirect ways, and they often choose to do so through play. Trauma triggers that occur during everyday life can also help children revisit trauma without overwhelming them. They might see, hear, or experience something that reminds them of a traumatic experience, and these triggers can awaken painful emotions, which, in turn, activate the natural recovery mechanisms.

I don't recommend either of the two traditional exposure techniques to help children recover from trauma. However, the basic concept of exposure therapy is correct: children must revisit the trauma in some way and become desensitized to it. The key lies in allowing sufficient exposure to elicit an emotional response but not enough to cause re-traumatization.

The healing process

To avoid hyperarousal or dissociation while revisiting trauma and painful emotions, children must understand that the present situation is *different from the original trauma* in spite of the similarities that they perceive, and that there is no real danger. There needs to be a balance between feelings of distress and safety in order for children to benefit from revisiting trauma. I call this the balance of attention.

To achieve this balance of attention, children must feel safe and protected in the presence of a loving and supportive person. When they have opportunities to revisit a traumatic experience while feeling safe and connected, they don't feel threatened and overwhelmed by the immediate need to survive, so they are less likely to become hyperaroused or dissociated. Instead, they are free to experience the entire range of emotions without blocking or numbing them.

Permanent healing requires more than simply being exposed to trauma triggers while feeling safe and experiencing the underlying emotions. The child must also have an opportunity to activate biological healing mechanisms during the exposure. When children become aware of painful emotions while feeling safe, their natural healing mechanisms are automatically activated. The final requirement for healing, therefore, is encouragement and acceptance of these natural recovery processes, which include crying, tantrums, trembling, laughter, specific kinds of play, and body movements. If the person with them accepts and encourages these forms of emotional expression and release, children will do what their bodies are designed to do.

As explained at the beginning of this chapter, posttraumatic symptoms occur because children become stuck in physiological states that are no longer adaptive. Healing from trauma allows children to become unstuck and bring the experience to its natural completion. The activation of these recovery behaviors while revisiting trauma in these gentle, safe ways results in a transformation of children's memories.

Revisiting trauma with and without emotional safety

Without emotional safety *Survival mechanisms activated*	With emotional safety *Healing mechanisms activated*
• Hyperarousal	• Crying, tantrums, trembling
• Dissociation	• Therapeutic play, laughter
	• Body movements

In Chapter 2, I explained that our memories are not static. In fact, every time we recall a past personal experience, our brain actively reconstructs it and then stores it in a slightly modified form. When children can revisit trauma and react to it in a more empowered way than they could at the time, their brain forms a new memory associated with feelings of safety, power, mastery, and completion (instead of feelings of terror and helplessness). These new memories replace the old ones and allow the child's brain to incorporate the disconnected sensory impressions and memories into a coherent, less threatening, narrative. By recreating the experience with a more favorable outcome, healing from trauma literally reprograms the brain to act as if the trauma has been successfully confronted and overcome.

To summarize, healing from trauma is an active process of desensitization and transformation, which requires revisiting the trauma in some way. However, the goal is not to relive the past (or even talk about it) but to focus on how children feel *in the present* when they encounter trauma triggers in everyday life or when they spontaneously revisit trauma during play. Two additional conditions must be met. Children must feel safe and connected when they revisit trauma, and they must be allowed to react freely to the trauma triggers with their natural biological healing mechanisms.

Chapter 4 describes how laughter and specific kinds of play

can help children recover from trauma, and Chapter 5 describes the therapeutic benefits of crying, raging, and trembling. Both chapters include information about therapeutic body movements.

Basic requirements for children to heal from trauma

- Feel emotionally safe and connected

- Revisit the trauma in some way

- React with natural biological healing mechanisms

Creating emotional safety and connection

Feeling safe and connected during a frightening event can prevent both hyperarousal and dissociation as well as the development of posttraumatic symptoms. Infants who are touched during stressful events show fewer physiological and behavioral indications of stress than those who have no human contact. A child who can cling to her parents during a medical procedure will feel safer and less threatened than a child whose parents are absent. If you know ahead of time that your child will face a painful or frightening event, the most helpful thing you can do is remain with her, preferably in close physical contact.

Sadly, we can't always be present when our children experience trauma, and we aren't always able to help them process the event in the immediate aftermath. However, we can create the emotional safety and connection required for them to heal later on, even if several weeks, months, or years have passed.

A first step is to help traumatized children feel protected from danger. They need to know that there is no longer any threat to their well-being or survival. One of the effects of feeling safe is that it allows children to feel emotional pain. When animals have acquired a conditioned fear response, studies have found that the conditioned stimuli for danger elicit numbness (analgesia). However, signals for safety inhibit the analgesic effect and actually *increase pain sensitivity*. Although similar studies have not been done on humans, these findings provide possible neurological evidence for the fact that feeling safe helps children lose their numbness to emotional pain. As explained in the previous section, this evokes the recuperative and healing behaviors described in this book.

Traumatized children also need to feel connected. Both hyperarousal and dissociation cause children to disconnect not only from their emotions but also from other people, the environment, and their bodies. Another aspect of emotional safety, therefore, is to help children restore all of these forms of connection. In order to feel connected to you, your children need your physical presence and loving attention. Eye contact is important, as is physical contact through touch, hand-holding, hugs, massages, or co-sleeping. Touch stimulates the production of oxytocin, a hormone that counteracts the stress response by reducing blood pressure and cortisol levels. Attachment needs grow stronger during and after trauma, so don't be surprised if your traumatized child needs you to stay with her at bedtime until she falls asleep, even after you thought that she had outgrown this need. If she refuses to play alone in a room, try to be tolerant of her need to keep you within eyesight. If you can postpone a business trip that takes you away from your child, it might be wise to do so.

Your simple physical presence may not be sufficient, however, because your children need to know that you are willing to support them while they activate the natural healing processes. This implies being available to listen to their entire range of emotions without distracting them or suppressing their need to cry. They need to trust that you are strong enough to tolerate all of their emotions and that nothing they say or do will cause you to reject them. If you tell your child to stop crying, try to distract him from crying, or put a pacifier in his mouth, he will feel that you are not willing to listen. Support for children's emotions also involves recognizing their efforts to heal through play and taking the time to join them in therapeutic play.

Even when you have established a loving connection with your children and have shown willingness to support their natural healing processes, children who struggle with chronic hyperarousal or dissociation may need additional help to connect to the environment and their bodies. During hyperarousal, children's agitation and distractibility prevent them from focusing on anything for very long, so they don't connect to their environment. During dissociation, children are calm but numb to body sensations, which contributes to disconnection from themselves, and their dreamlike state prevents them from connecting to the environment. When children disconnect in these various ways, they protect themselves from feeling, and this, in turn, prevents them from activating their natural healing mechanisms.

Sensory stimulation activities (especially tactile experiences) can counteract both of these chronic physiological states. Playing with sand, water, clay, or finger paints can help hyperaroused children slow down and take the time to notice their environment, beginning with these different textures. The sensation of tactile experiences can also help dissociated children emerge from their numbness and passivity and become more aware of their body sensations and the outside world. These activities can therefore function as gentle, non-threatening ways to help children regain the ability to feel and connect to the world. Most children willingly engage in these forms of play, even those who have been severely traumatized. After doing so in the presence of a supportive adult, children become more capable of feeling the emotional pain, terror, anger, or grief necessary to begin the healing process.

Several factors can decrease children's feelings of emotional safety and connection. If you use a punitive approach to discipline, this would be a good time to switch to a non-punitive approach. The use of punishment or any artificial consequences such as timeout will reduce your children's sense of safety, contribute to their feelings of powerlessness, and reduce their ability to heal from trauma. It's possible to set limits lovingly and encourage cooperation without being punitive. My other books describe a complete approach to discipline without punishments or rewards, so this topic is not covered in this book.

Your own emotional and physical state can affect your children's sense of safety. You will naturally feel upset if your child has been hurt or traumatized, and your child's trauma could also trigger your own unhealed childhood trauma. You can enhance emotional safety for your children by taking care of yourself and attending to your own needs and emotions. In fact, this may be one of the most important things you can do. You may need to do some healing yourself before your children will feel safe enough with you to begin their own recovery process. Look for a supportive friend with whom you can talk and cry. You might also benefit from taking time off work, finding household help, or hiring people to help take care of your children. Engage in activities that nurture and strengthen you, such as massages, walks in nature, music, or creative projects. If you decide to seek professional therapy, look for a trauma-informed therapist, and trust your intuition about the best approach for yourself.

Children who have experienced interpersonal trauma such as abuse may have difficulty feeling safe or connected with anyone, and almost anything can become a trauma trigger. Playful activities that incorporate touch and laughter can help, as described in the next chapter. With a sensitive, gradual approach, even highly traumatized children can regain a feeling of safety, trust, and connection, but don't hesitate to obtain professional therapy for your children if necessary.

To summarize, children know how to recover from trauma and will begin to do so when they feel safe, connected to a supportive adult, and connected to their own bodies and the environment. Feeling protected and connected enhances children's ability to safely revisit trauma without becoming overwhelmed, and they will then be ready to activate their natural healing mechanisms. Many parents report that their children "fall apart" (have a crying spell) when they arrive home after school. During a full day at school or daycare, children typically accumulate pent-up emotions from numerous frustrations, overstimulation, and mini-traumas. If your child remains calm at school but cries or has tantrums at home, it probably means that he feels safer at home than at school.

Indications of a healed child

Children who have healed from trauma no longer react to trauma triggers, and they don't suffer from chronic feelings of fear, anger, grief, guilt, powerlessness, or confusion. These children are delightful to be with. They are alert, with a surprisingly long attention span, and eagerly interact, smile, and communicate. They feel confident and enjoy learning, thinking, asking questions, exploring, developing new skills, playing, creating, cooperating, and contributing. They also sleep well and know what their bodies need. These children are gentle, kind, and compassionate, and they never intentionally hurt other people or animals. Children who don't fit this description are probably suffering from unmet needs, current stress in their lives, or unhealed past trauma. With the information in this book and with loving support, all children can regain their true nature.

It's important to remember that emotionally healthy children are not passive, and they don't necessarily fit the stereotype of well-behaved little angels! When parents encourage children to express emotions resulting from the inevitable upsets, hurts, and disappointments in life, those children don't use self-soothing habits (such as thumb sucking) to dissociate. Instead, they feel free to express the entire range of intense, but temporary, emotions such as anxiety, sadness, frustration, or anger. With this kind of daily support, they can maintain physiological homeostasis and avoid the extreme states of hyperarousal and dissociation.

Emotionally healthy children also know what they need and naturally persist in getting their needs met. This can cause them to be demanding and impatient at times, especially when they are too young to tolerate delays. However, this doesn't mean that they are suffering from trauma. Try to enjoy your child's vitality, curiosity, expressiveness, assertiveness, playfulness, and creativity, even though this may require much patience on your part. Be glad that these are signs of emotional health.

Natural Healing Mechanisms Part 1: Play and Laughter

PLAY IS ONE of children's primary healing mechanisms. I have identified nine kinds of interactive parent/child play that can help children heal from trauma as well as resolve behavior problems. I call these attachment play, and they are described in my book with that title. This chapter focuses on two therapeutic aspects of these nine kinds of attachment play: helping children feel safe and connected after traumatic events (a primary condition for healing), and helping children revisit trauma (a second condition for healing).

Some of these forms of play involve laughter, an important biological tension-release mechanism with many physiological benefits. Studies with adults have found that laughter can improve immune function, increase pain tolerance, decrease the stress response, and reduce anxiety. During the technique of gradual systematic desensitization, some researchers discovered that encouraging the client to laugh was more effective than asking the client to relax. Laughter can therefore help to restore homeostasis after frightening or traumatic experiences. These findings also apply to children. For example, studies with clown interventions in pediatric hospitals have shown that laughter can help reduce children's anxiety and promote healing.

Children laugh to release tensions caused by past traumatic experiences but also those that arise during new frightening events. In our efforts to get children to laugh, therefore, it's important to avoid activities that could frighten them. I don't recommend tick-

ling children or throwing them up in the air and catching them
even though they might laugh. Those activities could create new
anxiety or feelings of powerlessness. The playful activities described
in this chapter sometimes elicit laughter, but they accomplish this
without adding any new fears.

Play that helps children feel safe and connected

This section describes forms of attachment play that can help create
emotional safety and connection, which is a basic requirement for
healing.

Activities with body contact

Body contact is a powerful antidote to trauma. In the section on
creating emotional safety in Chapter 3, I explained the importance of physical contact such as holding hands and giving hugs or
massages. Games or activities that involve body contact can provide a fun way to create safety and connection. All traumatized
children can benefit from these activities, but they are especially
beneficial for those who dissociated and became numb during a
traumatic event. The tactile stimulation counteracts the numbness
and helps children become aware of their body sensations and
emotions.

Most children enjoy playful activities with physical contact,
and the possibilities are endless: hold your child in your arms while
dancing to music; lie on your back and raise your child in the air on
your feet while holding her hands; create a human sandwich by lying
on top of each other; do a group hug with your child in the middle; give your child a piggy-back ride while neighing like a horse.

Traumatized children sometimes resist being touched or held,
especially if they have been abused. Touch can make them feel
threatened and trigger a fight or flight reaction. A gentle, gradual
approach may be necessary for these children. You could suggest
hand-clapping rhythm games, playful activities in which the child
retrieves a small toy hidden in your sleeve, or silly activities in which
you place funny hats on each other's heads. A child too old for these

activities might let you rub sunscreen on her shoulders, give her a foot massage, or agree to a game of arm wrestling.

Traumatized children who resist all human contact sometimes feel safer connecting to an animal (such as a bird, cat, dog, rabbit, or horse) before they feel ready to connect to, and trust, another human being. Petting, holding, or feeding an animal has some of the same benefits as physical contact with another person.

Cooperative games and activities

Cooperative games and activities help children feel connected and confident. There are no winners or losers, so children can feel comfortable participating without worrying about the possibility of losing. You can play cooperative board games or card games with your children or modify competitive ones so nobody wins or loses. You can also modify many sports to make them cooperative. Ping pong and tennis can become cooperative games if the goal is to see how many times you can successfully hit the ball back and forth instead of trying to beat each other. Other cooperative activities include building a block tower together, creating a cooperative story or painting, doing cooking projects, making music together, or creating a photo album. Even cooperative housework can help children feel safe, connected, and confident!

You can also invent outdoor cooperative games that include movements such as jumping, running (but not races), climbing, rolling, throwing, or swinging. In addition to helping your children feel connected to you, these physical activities provide an antidote to the numbness and immobility which often follow traumatic experiences. They stimulate the vestibular and proprioceptive senses (detection of body movement and position), so they represent a form of sensory stimulation. Like touch, they can help children become aware of their bodies, an important prerequisite for feeling emotions.

Cooperative games and activities are especially useful for any situation in which there is stress, anger, or rivalry in the home such as parental divorce or sibling competitiveness. They are also helpful for children who feel stressed by a competitive educational system or competitive sports. Children who have experienced any kind of failure or defeat can also benefit from cooperative activities.

Nonsense play

Certain kinds of silly playful activities, which I call nonsense play, can counteract the seriousness of trauma while helping children feel safe and connected. These playful activities often involve intentional mistakes or humorous exaggerations. Let your children wear their socks on their hands, complete puzzles wrong, sing songs incorrectly, or place objects in wrong places. Children especially enjoy watching adults make mistakes, so don't be afraid to act playful and silly with your children.

Nonsense play can function as an antidote for any situation in which children feel guilty for doing something wrong or causing pain to someone else. It can therefore relieve feelings of guilt or shame resulting from trauma. Laughter during these activities helps children release stress and anxiety.

Contingency play

Contingency play is any playful activity in which your behavior is contingent on (or controlled by) your child's behavior. Imitation games such as "follow the leader" are a good example. Let your child be the leader while you imitate his movements and sounds. Your playful imitation will help him feel seen and heard, which will reassure him that you are paying close attention.

Other examples are games in which your child actively controls your behavior with commands. Let her pretend to be a king or queen while you play the role of a lowly servant and submit to her authority. You can also give your child a magic wand and let her put a spell on you to turn you into any animal she chooses. You must then obey her command by acting like that animal until she breaks the spell.

Another favorite game is "Red light, green light," in which your child stands on the other side of a room (or an outdoor area) and holds up either a red or green sign. When he holds the green sign, you are allowed to approach, but you must stop immediately if he switches to a red sign. A similar game is "Mother may I" in which your child gives you commands from a distance about how to move. He might say "take three baby steps," "take one giant step," or "take one step backwards." Before you move, however, you must ask, "Mother, may I?" (or "Father, may I?"). If he says "yes," you must move in the manner he has described, but if he says "no," you must remain immobile.

In addition to creating emotional safety and connection, contingency play can counteract the feelings of powerlessness that accompany all traumatic experiences. It is especially beneficial for children whose physical boundaries have been violated (by violence, sexual abuse, or invasive medical procedures). When children can control an adult's behavior during these playful activities, they regain a sense of power, control, safety, and trust.

Play that helps children feel safe and connected

- Activities with body contact

- Cooperative games and activities

- Nonsense play

- Contingency play

Play that helps children revisit trauma and transform memories

The following forms of attachment play help children feel safe and connected (like those in the previous section), but in addition, they incorporate ways for children to safely revisit trauma without becoming overwhelmed.

Nondirective child-centered play

In 1969, Virginia Axline wrote an influential book, *Play Therapy*, in which she introduced the concept of nondirective play. She discovered that paying attention to children while they play freely with a variety of toys can effectively help them. Researchers have since learned that this kind of play has therapeutic value and can even help solve children's behavior problems. The therapeutic value lies in the fact that it can strengthen emotional safety and connection while also providing opportunities for children to revisit trauma if they choose to do so. Children express themselves through play, so giving non-judgmental attention to a child who is playing is equivalent to listening attentively to another adult who talks about his life.

I advise parents to set aside 30 to 60 minutes at least once a week for individual nondirective play with each child in the family, even if the child has not been traumatized. A traumatized child could benefit from this kind of play every day. Begin by making a variety of toys and materials available to your child. These can include dolls, stuffed animals, puppets, a doll house with miniature furniture, small human and animal figures, small vehicles, a doctor kit, a pirate kit, building materials (such as a set of wooden blocks), modeling clay, art materials, masks, and dress-up clothes. Some parents set a timer and tell their child that they will play with him until it rings. Some call it "special time," "mommy time," or "daddy time." Avoid the temptation to answer your phone or do anything else that takes your attention away from your child.

As your child begins to play, don't tell him what to do or even make suggestions. Let him take the lead and play in any way he wants. You can share non-judgmental observations to let him know that you are paying attention, but respect his wish to play silently if he doesn't respond. Avoid directing, interpreting, teaching, correcting, or praising him. Join in the play but only if he invites you to do so. He might ask you to visit his imaginary zoo or play the role of a patient while he pretends to be a doctor. Maybe he would like you to draw a picture while he does.

With this kind of attention from adults, children often spontaneously incorporate themes of trauma into their play. Even children who avoid trauma triggers in real life and refuse to talk about a traumatic experience will often spontaneously revisit trauma through play in order to process their memories and emotions.

One of my clients brought her daughter, age two-and-a-half, for a play coaching session. While her mother and I both paid attention to her, the little girl chose to play with modeling clay. She created a nest with the clay and then rolled some more into balls, which she placed in the nest. She told us that they were dinosaur eggs. Then she found a plastic dinosaur among the collection of small animal figures and said that it was a fire-breathing dragon. She placed the dragon near the nest and pretended that it was breathing fire onto the eggs. I asked her what was happening, and she said that the dragon wanted to burn the baby dinosaurs, but they were safe inside their shells.

The mother and I found this play especially interesting in view of the family's trauma history. When the mother was eight months pregnant with the child, a devastating wildfire had swept through their city, and the family had only ten minutes to evacuate from their home. They escaped safely, taking only essential items with them. Sadly, however, the fire completely destroyed their house.

The mother felt amazed at her daughter's symbolic representation of the trauma and wondered if she had a prenatal memory of the event. Even without understanding the details of what had happened a month before she was born, her body had been affected by the surge in her mother's stress hormones and by her mother's frantic movements as she prepared to evacuate. The experience probably registered in the unborn child's own brain as terror. Also, she had heard her parents talk about the fire and evacuation numerous times, so she knew what had happened.

The child's theme of a fire-breathing dragon helped her revisit the trauma (reinforced through the family narrative) by re-enacting the event symbolically and maintaining control over the outcome.

Her statement that the baby dinosaurs were safe inside their eggs helped to counteract feelings of terror and powerlessness and create a sense of safety and successful survival, thereby rendering the family narrative less threatening. She may not have been aware of the connection between her play scene and the family's traumatic experience, but the connection occurred somewhere in her brain.

In order for posttraumatic play to be therapeutic, it must be interactive. Otherwise, it can become compulsive and repetitive. Sometimes traumatized children repeatedly re-enact traumatic experiences during solitary play without any therapeutic benefits. In 1976, a school bus full of children in California was hijacked. The driver and 26 children were held captive in an underground moving van for 16 hours until they managed to dig themselves out and escape. They had been terrified but physically unharmed. After the incident, one of the little girls repeatedly dug holes in her back yard, day after day, and buried her dolls in them. She did this activity alone, but her play never evolved, and it did not help her recover from the trauma.

Children need an adult present who pays attention, comments on the play theme, acknowledges their feelings, and actively participates if invited to do so. With adult attention and support, children typically talk (and sometimes laugh) during symbolic play, and the theme often evolves over time until it reaches a favorable outcome in which the child feels empowered. As children re-enact a traumatic experience in this manner through play, their memory of it becomes transformed.

Symbolic play with specific props or themes

When children suffer from posttraumatic symptoms but avoid trauma triggers in everyday life and don't spontaneously revisit trauma during nondirective play, they can benefit from suggestions for specific props or themes. If you know what event has caused your child's symptoms, you can suggest toys or a play theme that incorporate elements of the trauma while ensuring that your child feels safe and connected.

A helpful prop after hospitalization would be doctor kit. Your child will probably play with the toys in ways that help him heal from the medical trauma. A teddy-bear family can be a useful prop for any trauma that occurs within a family, such as parental divorce. A child who is terrified of dogs after a dog bite can benefit from play with a stuffed dog. Crawling through tunnels can help a child who had a traumatic birth.

At two years of age my son became separated from me and the rest of our family at a beach. I assumed he was with other family members as I walked to the bathroom, but they thought he was with me. He tried to follow me but lost sight of me and couldn't find his way back to the others. I found him crying and surrounded by adults who were trying to help him. However, my anger at my family (whom I blamed for not watching him properly) prevented me from supporting his crying at the time. He strongly resisted going to the beach after that day, so I suggested a game in which we re-enacted the event with small figures. He wanted to play it repeatedly, and he changed the outcome so that he didn't get lost but successfully caught up with me. After three days of playing our beach game, his fear resolved, and he was eager to return to the beach.

Children who are too old to play with dolls, stuffed animals, or small toys can revisit trauma, express themselves, and transform their memories through creative symbolic activities such as drawing, using modeling clay, storytelling, or role-playing. They will benefit most from these activities if a supportive adult pays attention to them.

Separation games

Separation games such as peek-a-boo and hide and seek are therapeutic for children who have experienced a traumatic separation, because they can revisit the trauma in a safe, playful way. The key therapeutic element in these activities is the joyful reunion that consistently follows the separation. The child knows that the parent/child connection will always be restored.

Babies begin to respond to the game of peek-a-boo after six months of age, which coincides with the beginning of a developmentally normal stage of separation anxiety. This anxiety is typical for babies who have formed a secure attachment to their parents. This game can be therapeutic for babies who have experienced separation trauma, especially during this vulnerable period of separation anxiety (which peaks between six and 18 months of age). Interestingly, babies in institutions who have not had the opportunity to form any attachments to adults do not respond to the game of peek-a-boo. During peek-a-boo, you briefly break eye contact with your baby by using your hands or a small towel to cover her face or your own. When you remove the towel and restore eye contact, your baby's laughter will help her release anxiety. Be careful not to prolong the separation, however. You don't want the game to become distressing.

Children past infancy who suffer from separation trauma can benefit from playing hide and seek, which transforms their memory to incorporate joyful reunions. If you hide somewhere and your child successfully finds you, he will feel a sense of mastery and completion because his active search results in restored connection with you. If you reverse the roles and your child hides while you search for him, his memory will be transformed by incorporating the experience of a parent who makes an effort to find him. In both cases, this game will counteract feelings of abandonment that the separation trauma might have caused.

A mother consulted with me about her four-year-old son who had become very aggressive and demanding after she had left him with his father and grandmother for two months. One of my suggestions was to play hide and seek with him as much as possible, and his behavior improved after she implemented my advice.

All adopted children have experienced separation from their biological mother, and those who stayed in an institution or temporary foster home before adoption suffered from additional separations. I have advised many parents of adopted children to play hide and seek with them on a regular basis. The parents usually notice a dramatic decrease in anxiety and behavior problems after implementing this advice.

Separation trauma can occur in the absence of a physical separation. If you are ill or depressed, you will understandably have less attention for your children, and your emotional disconnection can add to their anxiety. As soon as you feel better, you can help your children recover by playing separation games with them.

Regression play

Young children sometimes pretend to be a baby or a younger child. A four-year-old girl might pretend to cry, use baby talk, act helpless, or crawl around like a baby. This regression play often appears after the birth of another child, probably in hopes of obtaining the attention that the new baby receives. It can also be a way for children to return symbolically to their own infancy in order to re-experience a less stressful time when they were the center of their parents' attention.

Children also use spontaneous regression play to revisit trauma that occurred during infancy. Those who experienced early abuse, neglect, illness, or a mother's postpartum depression often initiate this kind of play. By acting like a baby, children can safely revisit their own infancy and any unhealed trauma or unmet needs that occurred during that time.

When your child of any age initiates regression play, resist the temptation to tell her to stop acting like a baby, and don't be afraid to playfully treat her like one. Sing lullabies, rock her, feed her with a bottle, bounce her playfully on your knees, and even put real (or imaginary) diapers on her if she wishes. Let her take the lead. Your child will feel loved, nurtured, and emotionally strengthened. If she is using regression play to revisit and recover from early trauma or unmet needs, your loving response will help to transform her memories of those early distressing experiences.

Power-reversal games

Power-reversal games are role-playing activities in which the parent pretends to be weak, frightened, or incompetent in order to allow the child to feel powerful. They can help children revisit, and heal from, specific traumatic events.

If your child has been bullied by other children at school, he would benefit from a playful pillow fight with you in which you fake weakness and fall dramatically to the floor each time he hits you with the pillow. His active body movements mimic the primitive survival behaviors of attack and self-defense, thereby completing the actions that were either ineffective or impossible during the playground bullying.

When immobility was part of your child's trauma (as is usually the case during medical procedures), an effective power-reversal game is one in which you sit on a chair and hold your child tightly between your knees while challenging her to escape. As she struggles to break free, you can provide some resistance at first but then fake sudden weakness and let her successfully get away. A variation of this activity is to reverse the roles and let your child capture you in some way such as locking you up in an imaginary cage or burying you under pillows. You make feeble attempts to escape but never succeed in doing so.

When fear is the child's primary posttraumatic emotion, an effective power-reversal activity is one in which he chases you while wearing a monster mask or attacks you with plastic snakes or spiders. If you respond by pretending to be frightened and letting him catch and attack you, he will feel empowered, and this will reduce his fear.

In addition to the body movements of attack or escape, laughter is an important aspect of power-reversal games. It indicates that your child is releasing stress and tensions associated with feelings of powerlessness, frustration, fear, or anger. Power-reversal play without laughter is not usually therapeutic.

Play that helps children revisit trauma and transform memories

- Nondirective child-centered play

- Symbolic play with specific props or themes

- Separation games

- Regression play

- Power-reversal games

Misinterpretations of children's attempts to heal through play

Even without awareness of the therapeutic value of these activities, most parents find them enjoyable and even initiate them. Sometimes, however, children's attempts to heal through play are not enjoyable and can be misinterpreted. In fact, your child's behavior could even cause you to feel irritated, angry, or frustrated.

One of my clients described an irritating behavior in her four-year-old son whom she had adopted from an orphanage in another country. He often ran away and hid in stores while they were shopping, which greatly annoyed his mother. Her son had been separated from his birth mother at birth and placed in an orphanage. At ten months of age, he experienced another separation when my client adopted him from the orphanage. I suggested that she frequently play hide and seek with him at home. She followed my advice, and he soon stopped running away and hiding in stores.

After experiencing trauma, your child might attempt to regain a sense of power and control by engaging you in contingency play that feels aggressive. For example, she might repeatedly poke you. If you respond playfully, you can turn her behavior into a therapeutic game and get her to laugh. Each time she pokes you, do something silly or unexpected (like jumping in the air or making a funny sound). You can even make different sounds or movements depending on which part of your body she pokes.

Children who cheat in games are sometimes suffering from experiences that left them feeling anxious, defeated, powerless, and incompetent. Cheating may be their way of asking for help. Instead of lecturing your child about the virtues of honesty, you might help him more by abandoning the official game rules and turning the game into a therapeutic power-reversal activity. If you pretend to be surprised at how well he is doing and complain about the fact that you are losing the game, he will probably begin to laugh and cheat even more openly. The laughter will help him relax while decreasing his feelings of anxiety and powerlessness. There's no need to worry that you are encouraging your child to cheat. After releasing his anxiety through laughter, his confidence will increase, and his need to cheat will probably decrease.

Children who are seeking connection might indicate this need in frustrating ways. For example, your daughter might stand on your feet and put her arms around your legs. You can meet her underlying need by turning the situation into a playful activity, perhaps by pretending that you haven't noticed her and expressing great surprise at how difficult it is to walk. Your child will probably begin to laugh.

A mother consulted with me about her six-year-old son who frequently fell on her intentionally while she was sitting on the couch. She had suffered from several serious illnesses and surgeries, beginning when he was a baby. These many long separations from her probably left him feeling terrified and confused. I suggested that he might be seeking connection but didn't dare ask for it directly because of fear that she would be too sick to hug him. I advised her to respond playfully by catching him in her arms whenever he fell on her and pretending that she would never let him go. I also advised her to play hide and seek. After implementing my advice, her son stopped falling on her.

When we interpret these irritating or obnoxious behaviors as invitations for therapeutic play instead of as misbehavior, we can respond playfully and meet children's underlying need to recover from trauma. Even when it's inconvenient, a few minutes of playful engagement with your child can help him feel connected and begin to heal. The result will be a happier and more secure child with fewer problematic behaviors.

Chapter 5

Natural Healing Mechanisms Part 2: Crying and Raging

CRYING AND RAGING are important healing mechanisms, which children do spontaneously after painful or frightening experiences. These forms of posttraumatic release help children rebalance their nervous system and transform their memories. In this chapter, I cover the therapeutic benefits of crying and explain how to respond to children's tears and tantrums in ways that enhance their recovery.

Spontaneous crying after trauma

Many studies have reported increased crying in children after traumatic experiences. Young children's crying spells and temper tantrums frequently increase for several weeks or months following surgery and hospitalization, even when there is adequate pain control. Birth is often one of the first frightening events. When the birth is difficult or complicated, with the need for medical interventions, babies can become traumatized. Babies who had a difficult birth typically cry much more than those whose birth was less traumatic. Even prenatal stress or trauma can affect babies. Mothers who were stressed or depressed during pregnancy have babies who cry more than those who were not exposed to prenatal maternal stress.

Observations of children following major disasters provide additional evidence for children's tendency to cry and rage after a traumatic experience. In 1991, researchers interviewed parents of young children in South Carolina after a devastating hurricane struck the area. Many parents reported an increase in their children's crying and temper tantrums during the months that followed the tragedy. Since that study, other researchers have reported similar findings about children who survived natural disasters such as hurricanes, wildfires, and floods.

Children who don't feel safe rarely cry. In the study (mentioned in Chapter 2) of young children who survived the 2001 terrorist attack in New York City, parents observed mostly hyperarousal and dissociation behaviors in their children on the day of the attack. However, they noticed increased crying and tantrums in their children for many months afterwards. They described their children as easily upset, highly irritable, and prone to tantrums. Some had nightmares and cried during the night for months. Many children burst into tears when they were exposed to trauma triggers such as an airplane in the sky or a loud noise. A four-year-old girl, who had been safely evacuated from the daycare center inside the World Trade Center, mourned the loss of her stroller (which had been left behind) and cried about it repeatedly for several months.

During traumatic experiences such as a natural disaster or terrorist attack, children may not feel safe enough to cry while the event is actually happening or during the immediate aftermath, especially if their parents are terrified, overwhelmed by grief, or busy dealing with evacuation efforts. In order to cope, children often dissociate. Later on, after the situation stabilizes and they feel safer, they typically cry spontaneously whenever they have an opportunity to do so.

A mother consulted with me about her two-and-a half-year-old daughter whose baby brother had died soon after birth, when the girl was 20 months old. Ten months after this tragic event, the girl became upset and cried when her mother read her the Christmas story about the birth of Jesus. The mother assumed that this birth story triggered her daughter's memory of her baby brother's death. A family tragedy such as this one is a highly destabilizing, terrifying, and confusing event for a young child. Unfortunately, the very people who could support her at the time (her parents) were understandably unable to do so. Not able to cry with support as much as needed at the time of the event, she made use of a trauma trigger ten months later in order to do so.

The experience of another client also illustrates the need for children to feel safe in order to cry. She told me that her eleven-year-old daughter normally cried as needed at home after hurtful or frightening experiences at school. However, the girl stopped crying entirely when the mother began to see doctors and was diagnosed with a serious illness.

These studies and observations illustrate that children spontaneously cry after traumatic experiences when they feel safe and that they make use of trauma triggers in order to do so. The following section provides evidence for the beneficial effects of crying and offers possible explanations for its effectiveness.

Benefits of crying

Studies of crying in both adults and children indicate that it can function as a homeostatic tension-release mechanism to restore physiological and emotional balance after a state of emotional distress. In one study, people who cried during a therapy session were physiologically more relaxed afterwards than a control group of people who exercised vigorously for an equivalent period of time. The measures of relaxation included heart rate, blood pressure, and brain wave patterns. In another study, adults who cried more while watching a sad film had lower saliva cortisol levels afterwards compared to those who cried less or not at all. Cortisol levels are commonly used as a measure of stress, so this finding indicates that those who cried had lower stress levels afterwards.

In an interesting study conducted many decades ago, researchers observed the behavior of children during the highly stressful experience of a long hospitalization. Children who protested openly by crying at the beginning of their hospital stay showed better adjustment later on than those who were quiet and cooperative right from the start. The latter appeared to be calm (a possible indication of dissociation) but were more likely to show signs of stress later on, such as regression to infantile modes of behavior (for example, loss of bowel or bladder control), eating or sleeping difficulties, anxieties, nightmares, and learning difficulties.

Emotional crying is a complex human behavior which helps children recover from stress and trauma, especially when they are lovingly supported. Several aspects of crying help to explain its beneficial effects: shedding tears, emitting loud vocalizations, performing certain body movements, and feeling connected to another person. The following sections explain how these four aspects of crying can contribute to its effectiveness as a tension-release mechanism and a way for children to transform distressing memories of trauma.

Shedding tears

Tear production is controlled by parasympathetic nerve fibers from the facial nerve, which stimulate the lacrimal glands to produce tears. The parasympathetic nervous system is also involved in dissociation (as explained in Chapter 2). However, dissociation is controlled by a different nerve (the vagus nerve), so the neural control of crying is unrelated to dissociation. In fact, crying does not occur during dissociation. Interestingly, the facial nerve also controls the muscles involved in facial expressions, which, like crying, are closely related to emotions.

Shedding tears may contribute to the tension-release effect of crying after trauma. A biochemical researcher, William Frey, detected the presence of stress-related hormones and neurotransmitters in the lacrimal glands and in tears (including ACTH, prolactin, endorphins, and catecholamines). These findings led to his hypothesis that one function of the lacrimal glands is to filter these stress-related chemicals from the blood and excrete them through tears. Shedding tears while crying would therefore help the body regain homeostasis. Frey's conclusion was that crying is "one of nature's adaptive responses to emotional stress."

Emitting loud vocalizations

Crying in human infants may have its evolutionary origin in distress vocalizations serving the purpose of survival. Physiological studies indicate that emotional crying in humans shares many character-istics and brain pathways with the separation cry of baby animals. The young of most mammal and bird species use high-pitched vocalizations to signal the parents (in most cases the mother) when they become separated and feel threatened. These sounds, known as the separation cry, attract the parents' attention and protection. This separation cry has obvious survival value because young vul-nerable animals who fail to alert their parents of their location are more likely to die from predators or starvation. Like the reactions of fight and flight, the separation cry in baby animals is an invol-untary, automatic reaction controlled by primitive brain areas in response to threat.

Human babies and young children, like baby animals, also use crying to signal their need for protection when separated from their parents (or other attachment figures). However, when they *continue to cry* in their parents' arms after all immediate needs have been met, it's clear that the crying is no longer functioning as a communication system to attract the parents' attention. Instead, it's possible that it serves the purpose of revisiting a past trauma and re-enacting the primitive survival mechanism of crying for help. This is especially therapeutic when children's crying during the trauma did not bring support or prevent the trauma, when they weren't able to cry, or when they dissociated during the trauma. Crying later on in their parents' arms can function as a correc-tive experience that helps them learn that their vocalizations *are* effective in bringing connection and protection. Afterwards, their memory of the traumatic event will be associated with feelings of power and protection instead of terror and helplessness.

Voluntary and involuntary body movements

As with body movements during certain kinds of play, the move-ments that accompany crying probably contribute to its ability to help children recover from trauma. Children rarely hold still while crying. Babies flail their arms and kick their legs, and young children typically throw themselves on the floor during tantrums while vigorously moving their arms and legs. These body movements use the energy that was mobilized by the hyperarousal response. They allow children to re-enact the survival mechanisms needed for defense or escape (fight or flight) and follow these strong motor impulses to completion. If the children were unable to avoid the trauma, or if they dissociated while it occurred, they may need to perform these movements of defense or escape multiple times while revisiting the trauma until their brain recognizes that the trauma has been confronted. These movements contradict the feelings of helplessness and physical paralysis that often accompany traumatic experiences. Children's memory of the trauma then becomes associated with feelings of power, mastery, and completion. These movements, therefore, complement the loud vocalizations emitted while crying. Both can contribute to the transformation of children's memories.

Shaking and teeth chattering sometimes accompany crying (or occur without crying), especially during and after experiences of extreme terror. Like deliberate body movements, involuntary movements such as trembling can help children release tension. Shaking commonly occurs when immobility or inactivity is the best (or only) survival mechanism or when a person feels threatened but trapped. When fight or flight is not possible, trembling can help release excess energy, prevent dissociation, and restore homeostasis. One theory of trembling is that it helps redistribute the blood circulation more evenly in the body after it has been diverted away from certain organs during hyperarousal (in situations when fight or flight was impossible).

Physical connection to another person
As mentioned previously, the proximity of another person is necessary for a corrective learning experience to occur when a child emits loud vocalizations while in the protective presence of

another person. An additional benefit of physical closeness while crying is the hormone oxytocin, which is released during social connection. This hormone helps to counteract the stress response and restore homeostasis. It acts on the amygdala to reduce fear, and it also inhibits the neural connections between the amygdala and the brain stem regions that play a role in hyperarousal and dissociation.

Crying alone and crying in arms are totally different situations from both a physiological and psychological perspective. The act of crying itself does not add to a child's stress, but crying alone can do so because of the separation from the parents. Studies of cortisol levels have confirmed this. One study measured cortisol levels in babies during sleep training, which is the practice of letting babies fall asleep alone even though they cry. Babies who are separated from their parents during sleep training have high cortisol levels *even after they have given up and stopped crying*, indicating that it's the separation (rather than the act of crying) that causes stress. Other studies have found that short separations from the mother in a lab cause crying and elevated cortisol levels in babies. However, if they are with an attentive and responsive person, their cortisol levels are lower even though they are crying. There is no evidence that crying in arms causes a baby to experience stress or an increase in cortisol levels.

Differences between crying alone and crying in arms during infancy

Crying alone	Crying in arms
• The baby feels frightened and abandoned.	• The baby feels safe and loved.
• Stress hormones are secreted (cortisol, etc.).	• Anti-stress hormones are secreted (oxytocin, etc.).
• Possible emotional damage.	• Emotional healing.

The implication from these studies and observations is that crying with body movements *while feeling safe with another person* is an effective way for children to release stress, restore homeostasis, and transform their memory of a situation when they felt unprotected and frightened. While revisiting the trauma, they use the energy mobilized by the stress response to re-enact the primitive survival behaviors (movements of fight and flight as well as crying for help). This new, corrective experience allows their brain to encode a memory of successfully confronting danger and bringing protection. Feelings of power, mastery, and completion replace memories of terror, defeat, and powerlessness. Physiological relaxation is enhanced by the shedding of tears containing stress hormones and by the increase in oxytocin during physical closeness with a supportive person.

What to do when babies and children cry and rage

Allowing your child to cry immediately after a traumatic event can prevent later posttraumatic symptoms. A mother told me that her two-year-old son, who didn't know how to swim, stepped into a swimming pool one day and began to sink. She immediately jumped in to rescue him. After they were safely out of the water, she held him in her arms while he cried hard for about ten minutes. He had no fear of the water afterwards and no other posttraumatic symptoms.

If a child doesn't cry at that time, however, he can do so later on. Children naturally strive for homeostasis, and they continually look for opportunities to heal by crying, although they might not do this consciously. They skillfully make use of trauma triggers that occur during everyday life. Whenever your child cries, your job is not to calm him down but to let the crying run its course while providing connection, empathy, safety, and reassurance.

How to respond to crying

I recommend always picking up your crying baby and checking for immediate needs before assuming that she needs to cry. If you suspect pain or illness, or if the crying seems excessive or has an unusual sound, please consult a doctor before implementing the approach described in this book. If your baby has no medical problems and continues to cry in arms after all immediate needs are met, it's likely that she is crying to heal from trauma or an accumulation of stress. Continue to hold her and allow her to cry while offering connection and empathy. Useful responses are "I'm listening," "It's okay to cry," "You're safe," "I love you," or "I will stay with you until you feel better."

The crying-in-arms approach can help babies recover from a major trauma such as a difficult birth or medical intervention. It can also help them heal from an accumulation of stress caused by daily frustrations, overstimulation, separations, frightening experiences, or unmet needs. Many babies have crying spells in the late afternoon or early evening when the stresses from the day have accumulated. Allowing your baby to cry in arms at bedtime can help her relax, regain homeostasis, and sleep well.

My son's birth lasted 48 hours, and he had many crying spells in my arms as an infant during which he vigorously kicked his legs and appeared to be struggling. While stuck in the birth canal, he must have felt frustrated and frightened, and he released his terror and frustration by crying in the safety of my arms while moving his body in ways that would have helped push himself out during his birth. He appeared to welcome resistance from my hands against his feet so he could push his feet against them to propel his body forward while crying. He was always calm, content, and extremely relaxed after those intense crying spells in my arms.

Try to resist the temptation to stop the crying with artificial calming methods. After babies have been fed, they don't need to continue sucking to fall asleep, so there is no need to give your baby a pacifier or keep offering your breast. I highly recommend breastfeeding for a year or more, but I advise against using your breast as a pacifier to calm your baby down when she is not hungry.

Most babies enjoy music and movement stimulation, but those are not immediate needs that cause them to cry, so it's best to avoid using singing or rocking in an attempt to soothe your baby before she has finished crying. She will benefit more from those lovely forms of stimulation in your arms when she is happy and alert.

You may have been led to believe that your baby must learn to fall asleep alone and that you must put her down before she is fully asleep, for fear of creating a bad habit. However, we are mammals, and all baby mammals seek closeness with their mothers while falling asleep. I recommend that you continue to hold your baby, even after she stops crying, and let her fall asleep in your arms before you put her down. You will not create any bad habits.

Some babies find their own emotional suppression habits, such as thumb sucking, in order to dissociate. When these behaviors become habitual, I call them control patterns. These dissociative habits often begin when parents try to distract babies from crying, leave them to cry or fall asleep alone, or don't provide the kind of attention they need in order to cry. Even if you carry your baby in a sling all day, you may be missing opportunities to encourage her to cry. If your baby has developed a control pattern such as thumb sucking, there is no reason to feel guilty. You can simply change the way you respond to her crying and offer connection, empathy, eye contact, and attentive listening at times when you think she might need to cry or when she begins to suck her thumb.

I have been teaching the crying-in-arms approach to parents for over thirty years, and parents frequently report to me that their babies are visibly calmer after a good cry in arms, and they also sleep well. Parents observe that the calmness after crying in arms lasts much longer than the state of mild dissociation caused by artificial calming techniques such as rocking or offering something to suck on. Babies whose parents regularly put them to sleep with artificial calming methods typically awaken after a few hours still needing to cry. Parents who practice the crying-in-arms approach at bedtime find that their babies sleep longer stretches at night. This approach differs from sleep training methods in which babies are left alone to cry (which I don't recommend).

As your child grows older, you can continue to support her need to cry. Sometimes you will know exactly why she is crying, but at other times, you may have no clue about the cause, even when she is ten or twelve years old. You can show empathy and help your child recover from whatever distress she is experiencing without knowing what it is. You may be eager for explanations, but this is not the best time to ask her how it happened (unless you need that information for medical reasons). Language and emotions are processed in different parts of the brain, so asking your child to talk instead of cry could switch her brain to a more cognitive mode of thinking while blocking her expression of emotions.

After your child becomes mobile, you can stay nearby and offer to hold her when she cries, but resist the urge to over-comfort her, and try not to overreact. A gentle acknowledgment of her feelings can be helpful. In the case of a physical injury, you might say, "It looks like that really hurts." If your child is shaking, hold her closely if she lets you, but don't try to prevent the trembling. Let her body do what it needs to do. Don't try to distract your child, cheer her up, or calm her down. Instead, stay present and supportive no matter how long it lasts.

You may be tempted to give your child advice, for example, by telling her what she could have done to avoid an injury or prevent a friend from being mean to her. However, advice is not helpful while a child is crying. You will have plenty of time afterwards to discuss these topics. Furthermore, children don't need as much advice as many people think they do. After crying, they often come up with their own solutions to problems or ideas for preventing them.

How to respond to tantrums

Sometimes children's crying seems totally out of proportion to the incident that triggered it, and they throw themselves on the floor in a fit of rage normally referred to as a temper tantrum or meltdown. When children have pent-up emotions from stress or unhealed trauma, almost anything can trigger a tantrum, and these triggers could have no obvious connection to a trauma. They function as symbols for past distressing events and provide a pretext for children to have a meltdown.

After a stressful day at school with multiple mini-traumas, a four-year-old child might find a pretext at home to have a tantrum. For example, he may burst into a fit of rage when his cookie breaks. I call this the broken-cookie phenomenon. You might find these kinds of tantrums especially difficult to tolerate, because it appears as if your child is over-reacting, totally out of control, or trying to be manipulative. It's important to remember, however, that stressed children who find pretexts to cry and rage at home are feeling safe. If they didn't feel safe enough to cry, they would become aggressive or find a way to self-soothe and dissociate.

I recommend staying with your raging child during a temper tantrum. It can be difficult to trust his need to release tensions in such a dramatic way, but he is doing what his body needs to do, just like urinating or defecating. It's important to give him space to thrash around while crying. His active body movements represent his thwarted attempts to fight or flee during experiences when he felt threatened or frustrated. You don't need to do anything to stop him, and he will benefit from your nearby presence, attention, and empathy. There is no need to hold him unless he wants to be held, but it's helpful to maintain some physical connection such as a hand on his back.

If your child has a tantrum in public, try to remain calm and supportive, although this may require an enormous amount of patience, especially if onlookers show disapproval. If necessary, remove him from the situation but stay with him until the tantrum has run its course. You can reduce the number of public tantrums by encouraging crying and tantrums at home, so try to notice times when you might be distracting or ignoring your child instead of welcoming his emotional outbursts.

A healthy tantrum does not involve violent or destructive behavior. Children who feel safe know that there is no real threat, so they don't need to defend themselves with violence. They naturally avoid harming anybody or anything during their outbursts. However, when children don't feel totally safe, they can become hyperaroused and violent. Hurtful or destructive behavior is always an indication of hyperarousal, not healing.

If your four-year-old son starts to hit his little sister, you will need to intervene, but simply telling him to stop hitting will probably not work. The use of punishment will not solve the underlying problem and will only give him more to cry about. The goal is to stop his aggressive behavior while helping him release pent-up tensions. One way to accomplish this is to engage him in a playful power-reversal pillow fight with you as the target (as described in Chapter 4), and encourage him to release anger and powerlessness through laughter and active body movements. If he still tries to hit his sister, you may need to physically prevent him from doing so. For example you can hold his wrists lovingly (but firmly) while explaining that you're not willing to let him hit his sister and that you need to protect her. This simple non-punitive restraint with your loving attention can help him channel his aggressive energy into healing tears instead of violence.

There are several steps you can take to decrease your child's aggressive behavior in the future: reduce sources of stress and over-stimulation, use a non-punitive approach to discipline, increase emotional safety, encourage spontaneous crying, and practice non-directive child-centered play with him on a regular basis. Please see my other books for more information about dealing with a child's violent behavior.

Misinterpretations of children's attempts to heal by crying and raging

In Chapter 2, I mentioned that it's common to misinterpret post-traumatic hyperarousal reactions, and in Chapter 4, I described how children's attempts to heal through play can be misinterpreted. Unfortunately, crying and tantrums are also frequently misunderstood.

Misinterpretation of crying in babies

Many people assume that crying during infancy always indicates an immediate need. It's true that babies cry to communicate their needs before they can talk. A hungry baby will cry until she is fed. But crying can also be a healing mechanism, and this fact can cause confusion. Even after you understand the two functions of crying during infancy (communication and healing) you may find it difficult to correctly interpret specific crying episodes.

Another misinterpretation is that crying during infancy indicates gas pain (colic). While some babies may have abdominal pain, studies have found that the majority of babies who cry extensively have no digestive problems. It's important to remember that frequent or prolonged crying is a typical behavior of babies who have experienced prenatal stress or birth trauma.

If your baby cries frequently, you might think that she was born with a difficult temperament. It's true that temperament can be determined by genetics, but many parents discover that their baby's temperament appears to change dramatically after they begin to implement the crying-in-arms approach. Their babies become calmer, less reactive, more cooperative, and more willing to be held and cuddled.

Many people assume incorrectly that crying is a symptom of hyperarousal and that babies are unable to self-regulate. When babies continue to cry excessively after all immediate needs have been met, you might think that your job is to help her "regulate" her emotions with soothing activities involving sounds, sucking, or movement. In the past, parents commonly gave their crying babies opium or alcohol to calm them down. However, babies are born with the ability to balance their nervous system, and one way they accomplish this is by crying. They need connection and empathy, but they don't need to be calmed down artificially.

Misinterpretations of crying during infancy

Possible misinterpretation	Correct information
Crying during infancy always indicates an immediate need.	Crying during infancy has two functions: communication and healing.
After all immediate needs are met, crying indicates gas pains (colic), teething, or a difficult temperament.	After all immediate needs are met, crying can indicate healing from stressful or traumatic experiences (including birth trauma).
Infants cry excessively because they cannot self-regulate. Parents should calm them with sounds, rocking, feeding, or a pacifier.	Infants know how to balance their nervous system by crying. They need to be held but not calmed down.

Misinterpretation of temper tantrums

During the Middle Ages in Europe, people believed that children who had frequent temper tantrums were possessed by a demon, and parents were advised to beat the devil out of them. Later, this belief gave way to one that attributed tantrums to a spoiled child's willfulness and stubbornness, and the remedy was to break the child's will with severe punishment.

Nowadays, many people still believe that children who have temper tantrums are misbehaving or trying to manipulate their parents. One commonly recommended remedy is still some form of punishment. Instead of corporal punishment, however, many books advise parents to withdraw attention from the child with methods such as time-out. A common non-punitive piece of advice is to distract children during tantrums.

Another current belief is that children who have frequent tantrums are not misbehaving but are suffering from a regulatory disorder or other psychiatric condition. The recommended remedy is often psychiatric medication, which may calm them down temporarily but not resolve the underlying cause.

An understanding of how children heal from trauma leads to a new interpretation of temper tantrums and a rejection of previous as well as current remedies. When you correctly interpret tantrums as healing mechanisms, you can play an important role by supporting your child and showing empathy. After the outburst, you will be rewarded with a child who is calmer, happier, and more cooperative.

Misinterpretations of temper tantrums
(Loud crying with active movements but no violence or destructiveness)

Possible misinterpretation	Correct information
Children who have temper tantrums are misbehaving or being manipulative and should be distracted or punished.	Children who have temper tantrums are doing what their bodies need to do and should be lovingly supported.
Children who have temper tantrums are dysregulated and should be calmed down or given medication.	Children who have temper tantrums are recovering from stress or trauma in a healthy way. Calming or medicating them could postpone their ability to heal.

Why it's difficult to support children's crying and tantrums
Many parents feel very uncomfortable when their children cry, and they are sometimes surprised at the intensity of their own emotions. One reason for this difficulty with crying is the mistaken belief that all crying indicates an immediate need. If you believe this, you will naturally feel frustrated, anxious, powerless, incompetent, or even angry when your child continues to cry after you have tried to meet all of his needs.

Sadly, crying is a major trigger for child abuse. However, parenting programs which emphasize the fact that crying during infancy is normal, and doesn't always indicate an immediate need, can be helpful. A study done in Canada showed that this kind of parent education reduces the dangerous tendency to shake a crying baby (which can cause brain damage).

Temper tantrums also commonly elicit feelings of frustration and anger in parents. Those caused by small, insignificant events (the broken-cookie phenomenon) are especially difficult to understand and interpret correctly because they appear to be unjustified. You may feel that your child is trying to manipulate you into giving him what he wants or that you haven't been strict enough.

Your own childhood experiences could also adversely affect your reactions. If you frequently feel anxious or angry when your child cries, you might benefit from exploring your parents' reactions to your crying when you were a child. Did your parents tell you to stop crying or punish you for doing so? Did they ignore you, dismiss your feelings, or distract you to keep you happy? Did they tell you that you were too sensitive? Were they abusive? If your parents didn't tolerate your crying, you had no personal experience of moving through painful emotions with an empathic listener. Your natural tendency will be to treat your children the same way you were treated, so if you lacked this kind of support and parental role model, you may find it difficult to tolerate your child's crying even when you understand the benefits.

If you feel a strong urge to stop your child's crying or temper tantrums, you could be attempting (unconsciously) to suppress your own anxiety, anger, or unshed tears. This self-protective attitude is understandable. However, a better approach for both you and your child would be to find a way to recover from your own childhood trauma and lack of support for crying. This will make it easier for you to help your child heal from trauma and become the kind of parent you want to be.

Chapter 6

Additional Tips for Helping Children Recover

IN THIS CHAPTER, I present additional information and advice for helping children heal from trauma. First, I summarize the important developmental stages to keep in mind. Then I delve more deeply into the topics of trauma triggers, re-traumatization, and the differences between calming techniques and healing techniques. In the final section, I suggest several other supportive measures that you can take to complete your child's recovery and help him regain confidence and joy.

Developmental stages

Children go through several developmental stages that strongly influence how they respond to trauma and how they recover. This section summarizes the main factors to consider when helping children of different ages heal from trauma.

Birth to six months

Infants up to six months of age heal primarily by crying in arms. Even if your infant has not experienced major trauma such as a difficult birth, he may need to cry frequently because of daily stress, frustrations, and overstimulation, which can easily occur at this age. Furthermore, he will be deeply affected by your own stress level, which can cause confusion and anxiety.

Preverbal infants also cry to communicate an immediate need, such as hunger or coldness, for which there is a remedy. When interpreting your baby's crying, it's important to check for all needs before assuming that he just needs to cry (including possible medical causes). He might also simply need to be held, in which case, the crying will stop when you pick him up. If the crying continues while you hold him, and if nothing satisfies him for very long, it's possible that he might need to cry in your arms.

Because of young infants' extreme helplessness, dissociation is likely to occur during traumatic experiences. They can also develop emotional suppression habits such as thumb sucking or self-rocking, even when there is no obvious trauma. These habits (called control patterns) help them become mildly dissociated when they have unexpressed feelings but don't feel free to cry. If your baby begins to suppress emotions in this manner, you can help by reducing stress and stimulation while increasing emotional safety and physical connection. Your baby will cry in your arms when he feels that you will allow him to do so.

Infants this age cannot understand symbols, which means that trauma triggers will occur only with actual sensory reminders. Triggers can include sights, sounds, smells, specific people or locations, body position, or internal body sensations. Those that occur in the context of everyday life can provide opportunities for your infant to revisit a trauma and heal by crying in arms.

Six to twelve months

Infants this age continue to heal primarily by crying. Before your baby can crawl or walk, I recommend always holding her in your arms while she cries. After she becomes mobile, it's still important to stay very close while giving her your full attention and empathy. However, it's okay to let her decide if she wants to be held. Your ten-month-old baby might prefer to sit on the floor next to you while crying even though she is capable of crawling into your lap.

Another developmental milestone during this period is the beginning of separation anxiety. By eight months of age, your baby might begin to show distress when separated from you. This anxiety indicates that she has formed a healthy attachment to you, and it means that a separation from you can be traumatic unless she is with a warm, familiar person.

During this stage, your baby will also begin to benefit from play and laughter. Effective play-based approaches include nondirective, child-centered play, separation games such as peek-a-boo, and simple contingency games in which you playfully imitate your baby's sounds or gestures or make predictable responses to them (such as saying "peep" each time she touches your nose). Any playful activity with body contact is also beneficial.

Symbolic play doesn't begin until the second year. Between six and twelve months of age, however, babies acquire the ability to imitate and to interpret adult imitations of real-life events if the props closely resemble real objects. This new ability offers a play-based option for helping babies this age revisit trauma in a non-threatening way. For example, if your baby has posttraumatic fears after falling off a bed, you could re-enact the fall with a doll to help her revisit the trauma and maybe laugh.

Twelve to 24 months

Strong separation anxiety typically characterizes this stage (whether your child has been traumatized or not), so separations from you will probably continue to be traumatic in the absence of a warm, familiar substitute caregiver. Crying continues to be the primary healing mechanism, and your child may also begin to have tantrums, which can indicate that a major trauma has occurred or simply an accumulation of stress and frustration.

Another typical behavior is resistance to caregiving routines such as diaper changes. This is a normal developmental stage, which requires much patience. In traumatized children, temper tantrums will be even more frequent, and lack of cooperation will be stronger. When children this age do not feel free to cry or rage, they may begin to show aggressive behaviors such as hitting or biting other children.

Healing through play and laughter becomes increasingly important and effective. A major developmental milestone by two years of age is the beginning of symbolic thought indicated by self-initiated symbolic play and the ability to talk. This new cognitive ability has important implications for healing from trauma. Your toddler may begin to revisit trauma through symbolic representations of trauma themes. By 24 months, your child will also benefit from most of the other forms of attachment play.

Two to eight years

Crying continues to be an important healing mechanism, and tantrums are common during this stage. Children often make use of minor pretexts to have a good cry or tantrum (the broken-cookie phenomenon). As they acquire more language skills, they begin to express their needs verbally, so you will probably find it easier to determine when your child's crying is a recovery mechanism rather than an attempt to communicate an immediate need.

Children this age frequently engage in spontaneous symbolic play, creating their own scenarios and incorporating elements of traumatic experiences. They also continue to benefit from all the other forms of attachment play. Your child will probably enjoy power-reversal games to counteract feelings of powerlessness through physical movements of attack or defense (for example a pillow fight in which you pretend to be overpowered while letting him "win"). He may also enjoy regression play during this stage, wanting to be treated like a baby.

Separation anxiety gradually decreases during this stage (unless a traumatic event has occurred). However, other fears might replace it. Your child's lack of information combined with a growing awareness of death can contribute to normal developmental fears, which are unrelated to trauma. These are also called normative fears. Typical fears include a fear of the dark, certain animals, thunder, bathtubs, toilets, and imaginary monsters. Your two-year might enjoy taking baths but begin to resist doing so at age three because of a fear of being sucked down the drain. Your child might suddenly become fearful of dogs even though he has never been attacked by one.

These normal developmental fears can cause confusion when trying to identify fears of traumatic origin. One guideline for distinguishing between the two kinds of fears is that traumatic fears are usually more specific, more intense, and more persistent than developmental fears. Children typically outgrow developmental fears without any intervention by eight to ten years of age, but traumatic fears don't usually disappear on their own.

This is the age during which children easily develop misconceptions and blame themselves for events beyond their control. Their thinking about themselves in relation to the world is egocentric, so they tend to exaggerate their own importance as a causal factor. Be sure to reassure your child that he is not the cause of traumatic events and that these don't represent punishment for something he has done wrong.

Eight to twelve years

Crying, play, and laughter continue to be important healing mechanisms during middle childhood. All the forms of attachment play can be successfully adapted to make them appropriate for your child at this age. Symbolic activities without real objects or toys become increasingly effective, such as revisiting trauma through artwork, storytelling, or role-playing. Your child will also become more capable of understanding, and talking about, the connections between her feelings and past traumatic events. However, talking and artwork do not replace the need to cry, and your child will continue to benefit from a good cry with your loving support. She may still use small pretexts in order to begin crying (the broken-cookie phenomenon).

Your child will have a more accurate and objective understanding of cause and effect and be less likely to feel responsible or guilty for causing traumatic events. Her early childhood fears will also gradually disappear. However, she may begin to express more realistic fears, such as worry about a terrorist attack or a wildfire. These fears that occur during middle childhood begin to resemble those felt by adults, and they are not necessarily caused by trauma.

Trauma triggers and re-traumatization

As mentioned previously in this book, anything that reminds children of a trauma can help them revisit it and provide an opportunity for healing, but trauma triggers can also overwhelm children and cause re-traumatization. If you worry that a specific trauma trigger will re-traumatize your child, it makes sense to avoid it. However, if you strive to shield your child from *everything* that elicits a memory of a traumatic event, he will never have an opportunity to activate his natural healing mechanisms. If your child refuses to enter a car after being in a car accident, you will probably want to help him safely revisit the trauma in order to recover as soon as possible instead of avoiding car rides. As with all aspects of parenting, helping your child recover from trauma will inevitably involve some trial and error, but a few mistakes won't damage him.

When to use trauma triggers

The ideal scenario is to create emotional safety and wait for spontaneous situations in everyday life to provide the necessary trauma triggers for your child to heal. Children often choose to revisit trauma when they feel safe, either through play or by making use of minor pretexts to cry (the broken-cookie phenomenon).

If your child is showing signs of unhealed trauma but doesn't laugh, cry, or spontaneously engage in therapeutic symbolic play, you can increase your efforts at creating emotional safety and then gently introduce a trauma trigger. These should always be used with caution. I recommend starting with the minimum amount of exposure necessary to trigger emotional arousal. A playful approach is usually the best way to begin.

Your intervention will be urgently needed if your child's trauma-related phobia or avoidance prevents her from eating, sleeping, defecating, or accepting necessary caregiving routines (being dressed, diapered, or bathed). If your child has been successfully potty trained but then has a frightening experience of an overflowing toilet, she might develop a toilet phobia and become constipated because of that experience. You can gently trigger the trauma by offering her materials with which to playfully re-enact the toilet incident through symbolic play (a doll, potty, and some brown modeling clay). If a playful approach doesn't work, and she continues to suffer from severe constipation, more direct exposure may be necessary, such as staying with her near the toilet while she cries.

Babies and toddlers sometimes reject all food after frightening experiences of choking, vomiting, or intrusive medical procedures involving the mouth or throat, and this posttraumatic food refusal can be life threatening. Tube feeding may be necessary until they recover from the trauma. Placing food directly on their lips or in their mouth can cause intense reactions and can be re-traumatizing. However, therapists have learned that babies (six months of age or older) begin accepting food again after watching an adult (a therapist or a parent) pretend to feed a realistic-looking doll with a miniature bottle or spoon. The babies sometimes grab the miniature bottle or spoon and bring it to their own mouth. This non-threatening portrayal of a feeding situation can help them safely revisit the trauma and transform their memories without actually being fed.

How to recognize re-traumatization

If your child is re-traumatized by a trauma trigger, he will indicate this by screaming in terror (hyperarousal) or by becoming unusually calm and unresponsive (dissociation). In both cases, he will disconnect from you and appear to be in a separate reality. Screaming could indicate physical pain or a serious medical condition, so you can't immediately assume that all screaming indicates terror. Please seek medical attention if your child's crying suddenly increases or sounds different than usual.

If you have ruled out medical causes and your child is screaming without connecting to you in any way, he may be in a state of re-traumatization and hyperarousal. Screaming in terror is different from therapeutic crying. The remedy is to provide physical connection, eye contact, and verbal empathy. If something in the environment has triggered his terror, you will need to remove him from the situation but stay with him. When he feels safe, the panic shrieks will give way to deep sobbing, which is *not* a symptom of hyperarousal.

If your baby closes his eyes while crying, this does not automatically imply that he is re-traumatized. Babies typically cry with their eyes closed while being held, but they open their eyes from time to time, make eye contact with the person who is holding them, then close their eyes and resume their crying with renewed vigor. If your baby never opens his eyes or always avoids looking at you while crying, keep trying to make eye contact. You can also gently caress his head, face, or arms and speak to him lovingly.

If your child is frozen in terror and becomes unresponsive (dissociation), the remedy is the same. Remove him from the situation, hold him, and try to connect visually and verbally. The goal is to reduce the level of terror and feeling of imminent threat. When your child feels safe and connected, he will become more responsive and begin to cry, tremble, or laugh in a therapeutic way.

Differences between calming techniques and healing techniques

Much confusion has arisen because of the incorrect assumption that crying indicates hyperarousal (the fight or flight response). This misunderstanding of therapeutic crying has led to the mistaken idea that parents should calm children down with soothing or distractions. As explained in Chapter 5, I don't recommend the use of calming techniques to stop babies or children from crying. From birth on, children know how to release stress, heal from trauma, and regain homeostasis. However, they must become active and emotionally aroused *before* reaching a calm state. While revisiting trauma, they need to experience a level of arousal similar to what they felt during the original trauma, release the emotions, and complete the urge to perform movements of defense or escape. They stop crying on their own when they are done.

Your role is to help your child feel safe, recognize her attempts to heal, and trust her natural healing process. Soothing methods can stop the crying and can put babies into mild dissociation, which is usually only temporary. It doesn't imply that the child is less stressed. Studies have shown that the use of pacifiers during stressful experiences such as circumcision decreases the amount of crying. However, it does not reliably reduce babies' cortisol levels, indicating that they are still stressed even though they are no longer crying.

We all want babies and children to be happy and relaxed, but it's not helpful to strive *directly* for calmness while bypassing the necessary active healing work. If unhealed trauma were a rotten wooden floor in need of repair, then calming traumatized children down without allowing them to express their emotions would be like covering the floor with thin plastic. The plastic coating would look nice and new, but it would soon wear off and reveal the rotten wood below.

Comparison of calming techniques and healing techniques

Characteristics of calming techniques	Characteristics of healing techniques
• Trauma triggers are avoided.	• Trauma triggers are used to revisit trauma.
• The child is passive.	
• The nervous system is calmed down.	• The child is active.
	• The brain is reprogrammed.
• Memories are unchanged.	• Memories are transformed.
• Emotions are suppressed.	• Emotions are released.
• Relaxation is immediate but temporary.	• Relaxation occurs later but lasts longer.

Although I don't normally recommend calming techniques for children, there are situations in which it may be necessary to suppress your child's crying with a soothing activity. If your child has a medical condition (such as a heart problem) for which hard crying would be a health risk, you will obviously need to keep her calm. Please consult with a doctor before implementing the advice in this book.

It would also be wise to calm your child down if her crying disturbs other people in a confined space such as an airplane. It's important to understand, however, that you are merely postponing your child's crying, and she will probably cry again at a later time.

If you or your partner are triggered by your child's crying and have an urge to hit or shake her, you may need to calm her down to protect her from the consequences of your anger. If this occurs on a regular basis, however, you and your partner will need to find therapeutic support.

Another situation when calming might be useful is with children who suffer from performance anxiety before an exam, oral presentation, or musical recital. These children can benefit from simple calming techniques (such as deep breathing exercises) immediately before the performance in order to function without panicking. However, if their anxiety results from a traumatic experience, these self-calming activities will not permanently cure their performance anxiety. They will need other kinds of support to recover from the original trauma.

Rebuilding confidence and joy

This section offers additional suggestions for supporting children's recovery from trauma. The goal is to help your child assimilate the trauma, minimize further distress, and regain confidence and joy.

Give correct information

An important part of recovery is to understand exactly what happened and why. Children, like adults, want to know why bad things happen. When they understand the reasons, they will be better prepared to face the future. Your child might want to know why he had to have surgery, why grandma died, or why the bad man shot people. Try to answer your child's questions with simple, accurate information in an age-appropriate manner, but spare him from unnecessary distressing details (unless he specifically requests these). It's okay to let your child know if there are aspects of a traumatic event that you don't know, don't understand, or don't wish to talk about. Be sure to tell him that the event was not his fault and does not represent punishment for something he did.

If a person or pet has died, avoid using the term sleep as a substitute for the word death. Children can misunderstand this term and develop a sleep phobia. It's also best to avoid the term "gone to heaven" immediately after a loved one has died. This statement can make children think that they shouldn't feel sad ("I mustn't cry because Mommy is in heaven.") If you wish to share your religious or spiritual beliefs with your child, try to do so in a way that doesn't confuse him.

If there was a specific perpetrator, explain that people who hurt others have almost always been hurt themselves. If the trauma was caused (intentionally or unintentionally) by someone intoxicated with alcohol or drugs, use the opportunity to inform your child about the impact of addictive substances on people's behavior.

Your child needs to know that it's okay to feel angry at whoever caused a traumatic event. Keep in mind that forgiveness cannot be forced, and children have difficulty understanding this concept. In fact, premature forgiveness can block the healing process, so don't ask or expect your child to forgive the perpetrator for his actions. Feelings of genuine forgiveness, understanding, and even compassion can arise spontaneously, but usually only after much healing has taken place.

For traumatic events that affect entire communities, such as a terrorist attack or natural disaster, tell your child who the helpers are (police, firefighters, doctors, nurses, etc.). This information can reassure him and help him feel less vulnerable in the future.

Protect your child from overstimulation and unpredictability

All trauma causes overstimulation, so it's important to protect trau-matized children from too much stimulation or too many new experiences. They need plenty of unscheduled free time. This may not be the best time to have your child begin piano lessons or join a soccer team.

Trauma represents a major change in children's lives, so they crave anything that feels normal. Familiarity and predictability can reassure them and help them feel safe. Try to maintain your daily routines and continue your family traditions and holiday celebra-tions. It's also helpful to avoid sudden changes in plans.

Empower your child to make choices and decisions

You can empower your child and build confidence by giving her choices and letting her make decisions. If she seems unable or unwilling to make decisions, begin with small ones and limited choices. Does she want to wear a red shirt or a blue one? Does she prefer to bring her stuffed bear or her rabbit to hold while riding in the car? As your child regains the ability and confidence to make small decisions, let her make more important ones, such as who to invite to her birthday party.

Be flexible about household rules, but don't hesitate to set limits

Some parents wonder whether they should be more lenient with a traumatized child and refrain from setting limits. I think it's important to be flexible, especially in the immediate aftermath of a traumatic event. However, an overly permissive approach can have disadvantages in the long term. You may eventually begin to resent your child, and he will feel less safe when he senses your resentment.

Reasonable limits can provide children with a pretext to cry, so if you hesitate to set any limits, you could miss opportunities to help your child heal. However, there is no need to use threats of punish-ment or promises of rewards. Those authoritarian approaches will only increase your child's stress and damage his feeling of emotional safety. I use the term loving limit to refer to those that you set lovingly without punishments or rewards and that can provide children with a pretext to cry. Limits based on what you are willing (or not willing) to do for your child can be especially effective.

A mother reported an example of a loving limit with her three-year-old son who was acting tense, unhappy, and demanding. He asked for a banana, so his mother gave him one. Then he asked for an apple instead of a banana, so his mother gave him an apple. Then he wanted his mother to slice the apple for him, so she did so, but then he started to cry because he wanted his mother to put the apple back together again! At that point, his mother stopped trying to please him and placed her hand gently on his back, saying, "I see you are upset. It's okay to cry. I am here with you." He cried hard for a while and then became visibly more relaxed, happier, and less demanding.

Create opportunities for success
To regain confidence, traumatized children need to feel capable and successful. Sometimes they accomplish this by choosing activities that guarantee success. Don't be surprised if your child prefers to read easy books or wants to do the old puzzles that she outgrew several years ago. She may choose those activities because she knows that she will be successful. Try to support her choices and avoid suggesting something more difficult. You can also increase your child's self-confidence by suggesting tasks that you know she can complete successfully. Would she be willing to set the table, help care for a pet, or make a birthday card for grandma?

Provide experiences of beauty and joy
The physiological reactions of hyperarousal and dissociation block not only painful emotions but also pleasant ones, which means that traumatized children are not able to experience as much joy as other children do. When children begin to heal, the awareness and release of painful emotions coincides with the emergence of

pleasant ones, and they spontaneously start to feel more joyful. However, they can benefit from additional support to accelerate the emergence of these pleasant feelings.

Begin by reassuring your child that it's okay to enjoy life even if something bad has happened. Moments of sadness, anger, and emotional processing need to alternate with moments of beauty and joy. The goal is not to distract your child from painful emotions or calm him down artificially, but to create a balance in his life. Think of yourself as contributing to your child's future pleasant memories.

Experiences in nature, such as walking in the woods or playing in snow, can be enjoyable without being overstimulating. You can add joyful moments to your family routine by watching humorous films together or scheduling family game nights. Sharing a meal, birthday, or holiday celebration with a few close friends or relatives can also bring joyful moments into your child's life.

Encourage self-expression through art, music, or dance

You can provide your child with art materials in case she wants to process aspects of the trauma through symbolic activities such as drawing, painting, or modeling with clay. Some children enjoy expressing themselves through music or dance. Don't expect all of your child's artistic endeavors to focus on trauma. She may simply want to create something beautiful.

I have personal experience with the benefits of music after a traumatic experience. One day, shortly after my twelfth birthday, I arrived home from school, and my mother told me that my beloved cat had been hit and killed by a car. I cried, of course, and my mother supported me in my grief. I was taking piano lessons at the time and had recently learned to play a simple piece by Schumann called *Erster Verlust*, which means First Loss. I enjoyed playing that piece during the weeks after my cat died. I found special meaning in it and felt supported by the fact that Schumann had composed something beautiful that expressed exactly how I felt.

Tips for helping traumatized children regain confidence and joy

- Give correct information.

- Protect your child from overstimulation and unpredictability.

- Empower your child to make choices and decisions.

- Be flexible about household rules, but don't hesitate to set limits.

- Create opportunities for success.

- Provide experiences of beauty and joy.

- Encourage self-expression through art, music, or dance.

With your loving support, your child can recover from trauma. The goal is not to make her forget about the trauma but to help her integrate the experience as part of her life story. She will learn that it's possible to survive a traumatic experience, move through the painful emotions, and resume her life with renewed confidence and joy. She will face life's future challenges with emotional strength and resilience.

Chapter 7

Case Histories Part 1: Birth to Five Years

IN THIS CHAPTER and the next one, I present some case histories that illustrate the various topics covered in this book. Many of them were submitted by Aware Parenting instructors who are raising their children with this approach and teaching it to others. To protect the identities of the families, I have changed all the names.

The purpose of these examples is to show how the basic principles of healing can be applied with children of different ages in a variety of situations. They are not meant to be copied exactly or implemented rigidly. Each child and situation is unique, and what works for one child might not work for another.

A five-month-old boy recovers from surgery and hospitalization

This first example is about the son of one of my clients. A longer version of this case was published in the *Infant Mental Health Journal* in 2007, and a follow-up study about the child's memory of the event was published in the journal of *Infant and Child Development* in 2008.

Description of the case

At five months of age, Michael had cranial remodeling surgery because of premature fusing of his sagittal skull fissure. The surgery was performed under general anesthesia and lasted about two hours.

Michael's parents were present with him in the hospital, except for short periods immediately before and after the surgery. They were allowed to take him home after three days in the hospital.

Michael cried at times in the hospital, and he sometimes attempted to resist the medical interventions. However, his crying and resistance were sporadic. He was weak because of the surgery, lack of food, and blood loss, and his throat was probably painful because of the tube used during the surgery. Also, the narcotic medication he received prevented him from feeling both physical and emotional pain.

During a catheterization procedure in which a nurse tried unsuccessfully to use a catheter that was too big, he screamed and actively resisted at first, indicating a hyperarousal response. As the painful procedure continued, however, he suddenly switched to dissociation. He became quiet and passive, but not asleep, as if he had given up attempting to escape.

After he returned home, his parents noticed a change in sleep, feeding, and crying patterns. Before the surgery, the intervals between night feedings had been as long as five to six hours. After the surgery, he began waking up as frequently as every two hours at night. They also noticed an increase in the amount of crying. He cried for at least two hours every day, even though he was being held and fed frequently. Some of these crying spells were in the middle of the night, when he would awaken suddenly and cry loudly. This crying occurred in spite of the use of appropriate pain medication for the surgical wound. He also began to have night terrors, something he had not had before. On two different occasions during his first week at home, he awakened in the night screaming hysterically without seeming to be aware of his surroundings. This crying was different from the crying that occurred during his other night awakenings, when he was awake and responsive.

The parents also noticed a change in his reaction to being placed on his back. Before the surgery, he loved being on his back to have his diapers or clothes changed and to interact with his parents. Afterwards, he often cried when his parents placed him in that position. Furthermore, he made no effort to roll from his back to his stomach, although he had learned to do so during the month before the surgery. He seemed to have lost that recently acquired motor skill.

An additional posttraumatic symptom was a new fear of strangers. Before the surgery, he had been interested in strangers and would smile when they interacted with him. After the surgery, he cried and turned away when strangers approached him, even though he was being held by one of his parents.

My recommendation to the parents was to hold their baby as much as possible and protect him from new or overwhelming experiences. I also told them to continue with the crying-in-arms approach, which they had been using since his birth. When he cried less than two hours after a full feeding of breast milk (either during the day or at night), his parents allowed him to cry as long as he wanted while comforting him in their arms. After crying in arms, he became relaxed and content, and usually fell asleep peacefully.

The parents expressed concern about the fact that he frequently cried when they laid him on his back for caretaking routines such as diaper changes. They wondered if they should allow him to cry in that position or if they should "rescue" him by picking him up. I explained to them that the supine position was probably a trauma trigger for him, because all of the painful procedures in the hospital had occurred when he was on his back, including the painful catheterization when he dissociated.

I encouraged them to experiment by leaving him on his back and supporting his crying in that position. The first time they tried this (one week after returning home from the hospital), they refrained from picking him up immediately after a diaper change. Instead, they left him on his back while touching him lovingly and speaking to him reassuringly. He cried hard for twenty minutes while frantically flailing his arms and kicking his legs. He then calmed down on his own. His parents picked him up and held him, and he fell asleep in their arms.

After that first session, Michael's night terrors disappeared, and he no longer cried immediately when his parents laid him on his back to change his diaper. However, he would still suddenly burst into tears for no apparent reason while on his back after a diaper change. Encouraged by the positive changes after their first experience of listening to him while he was on his back, the parents allowed him to have several more crying sessions while lying on his back with their loving attention. This crying was not always followed by immediate sleep. Sometimes he became calm and smiled at his parents after crying (while still on his back), and at other times he indicated a desire to nurse.

During the first month after his hospitalization, he had a total of eight intense crying sessions on his back. I witnessed and coached two of these sessions, which occurred spontaneously during consultations with me. On the tenth day after returning home from the hospital, the parents left him on his back after a feeding and a diaper change, but stayed close. At first, he responded joyfully to them but then suddenly started to cry. His father was on one side and his mother on the other, close enough for him to touch their faces. The parents touched him, looked at him lovingly, and spoke to him gently. They periodically picked him up to cradle him in their arms, and then gently laid him down again. While lying on his back crying, he looked alternately at his father and his mother, reaching out his hand to touch their faces. He repeated these head and arm movements every few minutes while crying hard for 45 minutes. He then spontaneously stopped crying, calmed down, and indicated that he wanted to nurse. His mother nursed him, and he fell asleep and slept calmly for about an hour, after which he awakened bright and alert.

A week later, he had another spontaneous intense crying session on his back with his parents on each side of him. He again looked from one parent to the other and reached out to touch their faces. After about an hour of crying, he began to calm down. His father held him and he fell asleep peacefully in his arms. He awakened after about ten minutes indicating a desire to nurse.

His mother nursed him, after which he was alert, cheerful, and responsive.

After that first month, he no longer seemed terrified of lying on his back and had no more crying spells in that position. He had regained his previous delight at being on his back for long periods of time to have his diapers changed, interact with his parents, and reach for objects. In addition, he regained the ability to roll over from his back to his stomach and even acquired a new skill: the ability to sit without support.

However, he still had some remaining symptoms. He still cried more than before the surgery, awakened frequently at night, and acted afraid of strangers. His parents continued to implement my original suggestions, including the crying-in-arms approach whenever he seemed to need to cry. By seven months of age (two months after his surgery), he had no remaining posttraumatic symptoms.

Comments

This example illustrates both hyperarousal and dissociation during trauma, as well as some typical posttraumatic symptoms. It shows how a spontaneous trauma trigger during everyday caretaking routines (being placed on his back) allowed him to revisit the trauma and served as a catalyst for therapeutic crying. He had been in that position during the painful catheter procedure when he had dissociated in the hospital, so there was a clear connection between the original trauma and the primary trauma trigger. During the crying sessions on his back, Michael became desensitized to the trauma trigger by learning that the supine position was no longer associated with pain and terror. His crying while feeling safe with his parents at his side allowed him to learn that he could cry and receive the protection he needed, and the act of crying helped his body regain homeostasis.

Michael's body movements probably also contributed to his recovery. His vigorous kicking and arm flailing while crying allowed him to do the fight or flight movements that had failed in preventing the painful and frightening hospital trauma. This gave him a sense of mastery and completion. Michael's repeated touching of his parents' faces while looking from one to the other also had significance, because post-surgery swelling of his head had forced his eyes shut in the hospital during the first day following his surgery. He must have felt terrified when he couldn't open his eyes to see his parents. Touching their faces while revisiting the trauma helped to transform his frightening memory of not being able to open his eyes and look at them the day after his surgery. If he had been a month or two older, he might have benefited from the game of peek-a-boo with laughter to help him heal from the temporary inability to open his eyes and see his parents in the hospital. At his age, however, attempts to play peek-a-boo might have re-traumatized him.

Follow-up study

In a follow-up study two years later, I asked Michael questions about his hospital experience while his mother was present. At two-and-a-half years of age, he was a verbally precocious child and was able to talk about specific memories of the experience. He even remembered that a nurse had been wearing a red scarf and had sung "Silent Night" to him, although his parents (at my request) had never discussed his hospital experience with him, nor had he seen any photos of it. He also remembered that he had vomited after the surgery and was unable to see during part of his hospital stay, although he didn't understand that his eyes had been swollen shut. When I asked him why he couldn't see, he tapped his eyelids with both hands and replied, "I closed my eyes because they hurt, in the hospital."

This study illustrates several aspects of memory. Michael's amazingly clear memory two years later of specific details from five months of age may have been made possible by the fact that he had an opportunity to process the experience soon after it occurred. At two-and-a-half years of age, the hospital event was obviously still a highly salient memory for him, but it did not appear to be traumatic. He answered my questions directly and without any apparent distress, as if he were describing a recent trip to a playground. Perhaps the therapy helped his brain process and store the memories of the experience without the accompanying painful emotions.

In addition to showing that children can remember early traumatic events, this follow-up study also illustrates the transformation of memories. He interpreted the memory of his eyes swollen shut according to his knowledge as a two-year-old with no understanding of the concept of swelling. However, he remembered the pain, so he assumed that he had voluntarily closed his eyes because they hurt. This supports findings from cognitive neuroscience research indicating that we actively reconstruct memories and transform them instead of retrieving them intact from storage.

A year later (when he was three-and-a-half years old), I interviewed him again, and he had no memory of the hospital experience. This suggests that there may be a window of opportunity around two to three years of age when children can recall and talk about traumatic experiences that occurred before they could talk.

A three-year-old boy recovers from a wildfire evacuation

An Aware Parenting instructor shared the following example with me about the effect of a wildfire on her son. I am reporting it here in her own words.

Description of the case

When Lenny was three years old, we had to evacuate from our home in the mountains because a wildfire was rapidly approaching. It was a very frightening situation. I was in somewhat of a panic, collecting the important items to take with us and talking to my neighbors about the best route to drive down the mountain. I told Lenny to sit down and wait for me while I did what I needed to do. A few minutes later, I looked at him and noticed that he was shaking violently. I was surprised because I had never seen him shake from fear before. I think he was very much affected by the fact that I was so obviously terrified myself.

We evacuated safely. After the fire was out and we were able to return home, Lenny was clingy and frightened every time he heard someone mention a fire. For many days afterwards, he cried and had more tantrums than usual. I suspected that his increased crying was his way of releasing tension resulting from the fire incident, and I encouraged and supported his crying.

He also incorporated fire themes into our play together. One time, we were playing with his dinosaurs out in the yard, and he asked me to make two of the smaller dinosaurs run away from a fire and act really scared. He pretended that one of the other dinosaurs was a firefighter who put out the fire with our garden hose (getting me wet in the process)! He had great fun doing this! He also became somewhat obsessed with fire for a while. He wanted me to light matches so he could put them out with water, over and over again. After a few weeks, he didn't seem to have such obvious fears of fires anymore, and his behavior returned back to normal.

Comments

During a natural disaster such as a wildfire, there is no perpetrator to fight against. The innate survival response is to outrun the fire, which is what wild animals instinctively do. In this case, however, neither fight nor flight were appropriate or possible, and the child's survival required him to keep still and wait while his mother prepared for their evacuation by car. The combination of the child's terror (amplified by his mother's terror), his forced immobility, and his natural urge to run caused his body to release tension and energy by trembling. Interestingly, it's typical for pet dogs to shake from terror during evacuations by car from a wildfire, likely for similar reasons.

This example supports the findings from many studies indicating that young children are likely to cry and have more temper tantrums during the weeks following a natural disaster. The mother, feeling terrified and preoccupied, was not available to offer emotional support during the evacuation, so he didn't feel safe enough to complete all of his body's natural responses at the time. After the situation resolved and his mother had more attention to support him, he finally felt safe enough to cry, and this crying helped him release the remaining tension in his body.

Lenny's desire to incorporate fire themes into his play illustrates the natural tendency of children to revisit trauma through play. He created situations in which he could extinguish both imaginary and real fires with water. These activities helped him process the trauma and transform his memory of feeling helpless and immobile during the wildfire.

A three-year-old girl recovers from a traumatic visit to the dentist

Another Aware Parenting instructor described how she and her husband helped their daughter recover from a distressing experience with a dentist. This report is in her own words.

Description of the case

Carla had just turned three years old. During a check-up at the dental office, she was found to have cavities in two molars, one on the right and one on the left. The grooves in her teeth were so deep that the cavities had gone unnoticed to us and had grown inwards. As they were almost reaching the nerve, we were advised to do fillings, and we scheduled two appointments a week apart, one for each cavity.

We were not able to prepare her very thoroughly for the first appointment because my husband was alone with both of our children, and I was absent due to work. However, we told Carla what would happen and that I would lie with her on the dentist's chair. We explained what a filling was, without going into details.

The day of the first appointment arrived. After a few minutes in the waiting room, we went into the dentist office and I lay down on the chair with Carla on top of me. There were three people with us, two of whom we had never met before. The first thing they did was to apply a local anesthetic cream on Carla's gums. They told her it would taste like banana, but Carla didn't like the taste, and from then on, she had a hard time trusting what they told her. Next, they injected an anesthetic and began to prepare the area for the filling.

Then they placed surgical bands and rings in her mouth to isolate the working area. Carla reacted by moving her arms and legs uncontrollably. They asked me to restrain her so she would not hit the equipment and so they could proceed with their work. From then on, Carla started crying and trying to break free to escape, and she didn't stop struggling until the procedure was over. I had to hold her tightly while the dentist and assistants told her that it was nothing, that it would only last a moment, that she should hold still, and that she shouldn't cry. They did not always speak to her kindly. The intervention was very quick, but for me it felt like forever.

When it was all over, they warned me that the next appointment would probably be worse now that Carla knew what would happen. They told me that they were not sure they could do the second filling unless we gave her a muscle relaxant to prevent her from struggling.

When we left the dental office, Carla was still crying, so I looked for a quiet place where I could sit with her on my lap and support her crying. She fell asleep after about ten minutes, so I took her to the car and then back home. When she woke up, she didn't look like herself. She was dull, sleepy, slow to answer when I spoke to her, and didn't seem to have her usual energy or enough strength to move normally. We spent several hours on the couch cuddled together, resting. I had never seen her like this. My whole body ached from the effort I had made to hold her still during the procedure, and I began to think that in seven days we had to go back to do the filling on the other side. How were we going to manage?

My husband and I decided to use attachment play to help Carla recover from the experience and also prepare for the next appointment. Each day during the week, we suggested symbolic play with the theme of being at the dentist, and we did this activity several times a day. The first few days, she only wanted to play the role of the dentist, not the patient. She stuffed rags into our mouths until they no longer fit. She used a small flashlight to examine our mouths, and she pretended to use various instruments to do fillings. We pretended to dislike it and we protested, but we let her do it. Later the game evolved, and she played the role of the patient. I received her in the consulting room, introduced myself, sat her on the chair and asked her to wait while I prepared the anesthetic, while strongly insisting that she should stay there. But every time I came back with the anesthetic, she had managed to escape. Sometimes she would hide, and I would pretend to be desperate looking for her while she kept laughing. At other times, she imagined a fairy who came in through the window, paralyzed me with her magic wand, and helped her escape.

The game was revealing for us because it helped us understand how she had experienced the procedure. For example, during our first few games, she put rags in our mouths. She later told us that what scared her the most was the choking sensation caused by the surgical bands and the fact that she wasn't able to swallow normally.

As the time for the second appointment approached, we talked about each step of the procedure to find out how she had felt and to work together to find ways to cope better the second time. We agreed that I would hold her gently to prevent her from moving her hands impulsively to avoid accidents. We agreed on different signals that she could use to let me know when she needed to swallow or if she was in pain and needed a break. We invented our own terms to refer to the nurses (she called them "poopy nurse"), and we became accomplices. I don't think those conversations would have been possible without the play, and both contributed to making the second experience so much better.

We arrived at the clinic for the second appointment and were led into the waiting room. When the nurse came in and called her name, Carla took a step back while covering her mouth. I crouched down in front of her and held my arms out to her. She wrapped her arms around me and let me carry her to the dentist chair. Once there, I held her all the time, but there was no need to restrain her, and she didn't try to escape. She fully cooperated at all times while tears rolled silently down her cheeks and her leg beat rhythmically against the chair. When the procedure was finished, the three dentists were speechless with amazement at how well she had cooperated! That afternoon, Carla had a good cry, and when she finished crying, she was as joyful, talkative, and playful as usual.

Comments

Carla's resistance during the first dental appointment illustrates hyperarousal during a traumatic experience. She protested and physically resisted the procedure, and she had to be forcefully restrained. Following the procedure, she began the healing process by crying with her mother's support, but she soon fell asleep. Her sudden sleepiness and unusual lethargic behavior after awakening indicate posttraumatic dissociation.

This example also illustrates the effectiveness of symbolic play with the trauma theme. By playing the role of the dentist and then the patient, Carla was able to revisit the trauma while feeling safe. The game became a power-reversal game in which the parents made feeble attempts to resist while Carla did to them what had most frightened her. While playing the role of the patient, she greatly enjoyed physically escaping from the dentist, which is what she had tried unsuccessfully to do during the actual procedure. She also created an imaginary fairy who helped her escape. Playing the role of a patient who successfully escapes was also a power-reversal game, because the parents pretended to be incapable of preventing her from getting away.

These experiences all helped Carla transform her memory and reprogram her brain to think that she had successfully confronted the perceived threat. Her memory of the experience became associated with feelings of power and successful escape. Her laughter during the play helped her release tensions and restore homeostasis. The preparation for the second procedure through play further helped her to feel powerful and in control of the situation. It is not surprising that she fully cooperated during the second procedure.

Two of her behaviors during the second procedure helped her maintain homeostasis: shedding silent tears and beating her leg rhythmically against the chair. The tears and silent crying helped her release tensions, and the rhythmical beating of her leg helped her release some of the energy mobilized for fight or flight but without actually attempting to escape. In this manner, she was able to tolerate the procedure without going into hyperarousal or dissociation. Her crying later that day helped her release residual emotions from both procedures and complete her recovery.

A four-year-old girl recovers from her parents' divorce

Another Aware Parenting instructor shared how her divorce affected her daughter and how she helped her recover. This report is in her own words.

Description of the case

My oldest daughter, Elena, was four-and-a-half years old when her father told her that he was going to move out of the house. We were at the beach, and she threw sand furiously in his face and wanted to leave the place immediately. After our divorce, there was a huge increase in her crying, tantrums, separation anxiety, nightmares, and sleep problems.

I created emotional safety by providing a lot of physical closeness during the day and at night. I was available to accept her whole range of intense emotions so she could release the emotional pain and tension in her body as soon as possible. I told her, "It's okay to cry, honey. I am right here with you, and I will not leave you alone with those big feelings. You are safe and protected with me. You can cry as long as you want. You don't need to explain anything to me."

I did several play sessions with her using a teddy bear family just like our own. I explained that the mommy bear and the daddy bear had a hard time agreeing on things, so it was better for the whole family that they live in different places. I told her that even though they don't live together any more, they still love their daughters. When we played with the bears at the beach, Elena took the child bear representing herself and had it throw sand in the daddy bear's face. She even buried the daddy bear under the sand, which was a huge source of amusement and laughter for her (and also for me). She was always more relaxed and connected after these play sessions. I also brought her to a professional therapist for a few sessions.

Two years have passed since I got divorced, and she has regained confidence and joy. Her crying, tantrums, separation anxiety, and nightmares have all decreased. She also sleeps much more soundly.

Comments

In this example, the child's initial reaction was aggression towards her father and a desire to escape from the situation (hyperarousal reaction). The mother helped her daughter heal by creating emotional safety, accepting her crying and tantrums, and engaging her in symbolic play with laughter. The girl was able to express her emotions by attacking and burying the teddy bear father.

The mother was directly implicated in this trauma, so she was wise to seek professional therapy for her daughter. For trauma that occurs within a family (such as divorce), it can be helpful to seek support from someone who is not emotionally involved.

Chapter 8

Case Histories Part 2: Six to Twelve Years

A six-year-old boy recovers from a serious accident

A psychotherapist, also trained in Aware Parenting, shared the following example with me about one of her clients, which I have summarized.

Description of the case

Her client, a six-year-old boy, had been encouraged by his father to try using a zip-line. These kinds of zip-lines, common in some European countries, are built on the slope of a hill or mountain. The person must climb up to a platform, grab onto a bar, and hold on while coasting down the wire. There is no safety harness. The boy felt terrified and resisted at first, but his father insisted that he should give it a try. Wanting to please his father, the boy did so. Unfortunately, he failed to grab the bar securely and fell to the ground, sustaining multiple fractures in his arm, leg, and jaw, as well as several broken teeth. There was much commotion right after the accident. The adults around him began screaming, and he was rushed to the hospital in an ambulance.

After surgery and hospitalization, he was allowed to recuperate in a special hospital bed installed in the family's living room. His mother slept near him, but she hardly got any sleep because he suffered from night terrors every night, screaming, "No, Daddy, no." He reported recurring dreams of falling into a hole with a bear at the bottom that was about to devour him. She set up an appointment with the therapist and explained the situation to her.

The therapist visited the boy in his home bringing with her a long string and a teddy bear family. She attached one end of the string to a high lamp and the other end to the railing of the child's bed. Under the string, she placed soft pillows on the floor. With the mother present, the therapist re-enacted the zip-line accident by having the small teddy bear (representing the child) climb up with trepidation to the high end of the string while the big teddy bear (representing the father) helped push him up. She also re-enacted the little bear's fall but did not make him get hurt. Instead, she floated him downwards in slow motion and landed him safely on the soft pillows. The child (who was in the bed) paid close attention and laughed while watching the little bear land safely. She repeated the re-enactment several times while the child laughed heartily each time. After that therapy session, the child's nightmares and night terrors disappeared.

In a second session, the father was present, and the boy wanted to repeat the zip-line re-enactment with the bears. This time, the therapist had the small bear successfully coast down the zip-line without falling. While watching the re-enactment, the child wanted his father to sit next to him on his bed. Then the therapist placed the string on the floor in a long line about two meters from the child's bed and parallel to it, creating a symbolic barrier. She went to the other side of the room and slowly walked towards the string, instructing the child to prevent her from crossing over it by saying "stop" and making firm hand and arm gestures like a policeman controlling traffic. The boy always stopped her with loud words and strong gestures before she crossed over the string. Then she invited the father to participate and told him to obey his son's commands while approaching the string. The boy said "stop" immediately to his father after only one step forward. They repeated the game several times, much to the child's delight, and he never allowed his father to take more than one step forward.

In a third session, the therapist used play to prepare the child for a post-surgery check-up at the hospital. The child had expressed reluctance to return there, and the mother feared that her son's resistance and lack of cooperation would prevent her from bringing him to the appointment. The therapist dressed like a doctor and used a humorous name, which made the child laugh. Then he wanted to play the role of the doctor, so the therapist played the role of the child and protested loudly while the mother tried to bring her to the doctor. The child laughed heartily during this play. The mother later reported that the hospital visit took place with no problem. The child cooperated willingly with the four specialists he saw and even drew a picture for each of them.

Comments

This child could have processed some of the trauma by crying and trembling immediately after his fall if someone had been available to support him. Unfortunately, he didn't have an opportunity to do so at that time because the adults around him were screaming and panicking, which probably only added to his terror. They were understandably more concerned about his need for immediate medical interventions than his need for emotional support. His posttraumatic symptoms included nightmares, night terrors, anger at his father, and fear of returning to the hospital.

The therapist used four different kinds of attachment play to help the child revisit the trauma and regain a sense of power and control. First, she used symbolic play with a teddy bear to re-enact the zip-line incident but with some important differences. She initially created a soft landing, then a successful ride down the zip-line. Even though the child was not able to actively participate (because he was bed-ridden), he was able to do so vicariously by watching, and this was effective.

The therapist then used contingency play (obeying the child's instructions to stop) to help him regain a sense of power and control over his father (whom he blamed for the accident by insisting that he try the zip-line). She also used nonsense play (pretending to be a doctor with a silly name) to help him feel safe and laugh.

Finally, she used power-reversal play (letting him be the doctor while she played the role of a frightened child) to revisit the experience of frightening and painful medical procedures while allowing him to laugh and feel powerful.

These play experiences helped the child transform his memory of the trauma, repair his relationship with his father, and release anxiety and tensions through laughter. The disappearance of nightmares and night terrors and his willingness to return to the hospital for a follow-up visit indicated that the therapy was effective. An unexpected positive change also occurred after the second session. The physical therapist who visited him later that day noticed that the boy had suddenly regained normal movement in his injured leg, which had previously been stiff and stuck in one position. This change indicated that the boy had released tension from his body.

Although the playful therapeutic approaches described in this case were done by a professional psychotherapist, the child's parents could also have implemented them.

A seven-year-old boy recovers from a frightening incident at school

Another Aware Parenting instructor shared the following incident with me. This report is in her own words.

Description of the case

When my son was seven years old, a frightening incident occurred at his school. He found a used hypodermic syringe on the playground. In spite of the information that I had given him about not touching such things, he picked it up and took it to a classroom teacher. The teacher let out a screech and yelled, "Drop it!" The school staff then disposed of the syringe and let me know about the incident.

That afternoon, my son came home and found a toy syringe that we had in a doctor kit. He asked me to play with him and two dolls. I watched as he played out the incident that had occurred at school that day. He exaggerated the event and laughed about it. I thought he had released the stress from the day's events, and the evening went on as normal.

However, that night he couldn't sleep. He came out of his bedroom to sit with me on the couch. I encouraged him to draw a picture about his day. He drew a picture about the events that had happened that day, including details such as facial expressions and emotions. He had not yet cried about what had happened, and I said to him, "It's okay to cry if you need to." He began to cry as I held him. Neither of us spoke while he cried, and I silently accepted his tears. When he felt ready, he went back to bed and fell asleep easily.

Comments

This example demonstrates how children can become traumatized by an adult's reaction to an event. If the teacher had reacted more calmly, the boy would probably not have been traumatized. Instead, she panicked, screamed, and yelled at him.

The boy knew what he needed to do in order to recover. He used props from a doctor kit to revisit the trauma and process the experience. His playful exaggerations allowed him to laugh and release tensions. At bedtime, when he needed more support, the mother suggested drawing as another way for him to revisit the trauma. Her permission for him to cry further helped him release tensions and relax enough to fall asleep.

A seven-year-old girl recovers from sexual abuse

The following report is from an Aware Parenting instructor whose daughter had been sexually abused. The mother described her daughter's recovery during the three years following the abuse.

Description of the case

My daughter, Ida, was seven years old when we learned that she had been sexually abused. We had welcomed a 16-year-old boy into our family, and he had involved her in secret sexual behavior for about four months before we learned about it. Our entire family was traumatized by this incident, and we are still processing it (three years later). I cannot emphasize enough how much Aware Parenting has helped us.

While the abuse was going on, we noticed several behavioral changes in Ida. She was frequently angry, rude, and aggressive. She was nervous and restless in her body. She often moved her body back and forth while humming. She also started to wet the bed and was more afraid at night. She avoided spending time with me, and when I planned moments alone with her, she was quiet and withdrawn. She kept saying that nothing was wrong or bothering her.

From the moment we were aware of the abuse, Ida was able to share about what had been happening. She was very angry when she realized that the boy had been lying to her by telling her that we wouldn't be angry at all if we found out what they were doing. During the two months that followed, she told me several times that there was more that she wanted to talk about, but I needed to ask questions while she answered yes or no. She avoided eye-contact and felt ashamed. After I learned what she wanted to share with me, she would open up and talk more.

She had difficulty going to sleep for weeks. She was afraid that the boy would come back and get very mad at her for sharing their secret with us. A big trauma trigger for her was seeing teenage boys. She would turn pale, become tense, and her body would freeze. She continued to wet the bed and have nightmares for several months, and she wanted to be close to us. We chose to report the abuse to the police, and they interviewed her for two hours. After the interview, she jumped cheerfully into my arms and felt relieved.

Then Ida started to have violent tantrums every other day for a year and a half. Before each of her tantrums, we could all see and feel it coming. She became grumpy and frustrated and started to get irritated with us or her brothers. Then she would quickly become angry and start throwing things, yelling, kicking, and hitting. We cleared a spot in the bedroom where she could have her tantrums in safety while I stayed with her. Sometimes she walked in there herself, and sometimes I carried her there. She often directed her anger at me, and it was a physical struggle to stop her from hurting me. I was calm and clear with my boundaries, and I gave her my full attention. I encouraged her to let it out. Sometimes she threw herself on the bed and thrashed around very actively, moving her arms and legs while screaming into a pillow. After about five or ten minutes, she would curl up in my arms and start to cry in a calmer way. She told me she loved me, and her breathing would become calmer. She indicated when she felt ready to go back to the other room.

I was able to do this only because I took care of my own emotional needs. I screamed, cried, and had my own tantrums at separate times (alone, with my husband, or with a very close friend). We talked with her about her tantrums and let her know that her body knew exactly what it needed to do in order to heal.

She was very curious about being in love, kissing, and sexuality. She liked to look at books with me about these topics and ask all kinds of questions. We discussed respect for our own and other people's bodies. We were living in a warm climate, and we noticed that she felt free to be naked around us, and there was nothing sexual about that.

We encouraged laughter by making jokes about sending packages of poo to her abuser. She enjoyed drawing pictures of him naked, drawing his penis, and then burning the drawings while laughing really hard. She initiated a game with her two younger brothers in which I was an angry monster mama who tried to catch them but never succeeded. They all laughed during this game and still enjoy playing it.

At first, she wanted someone with her at all times because she was scared, so we stayed with her. But then we began to encourage her to do things on her own, starting with going upstairs alone to get something in her room, then visiting a neighbor friend. We always acknowledged her fear, and she slowly conquered it.

She has shared her experience with a few people. Most of the women she chose to talk to had also been sexually abused as a child.

She also talked about it with her aunt and grandmother. She would like to meet another girl her age who has experienced the same thing, but this hasn't happened yet.

She still (three years after the abuse) tells me when she needs to have some time with me so I can explain again what I shared with the police. She wants to talk about what happened and ask questions. She sits close to me and pulls my arms around her. She uses a special decorated stone that she puts in a chosen spot in the living room to indicate when she needs time with us alone to talk about abuse-related stuff. Recently, she has started using the stone to indicate when she wants to talk about other things as well.

Until recently, she has been playing with dolls and taking care of them, being very kind and loving with them. She asked for a big doll for her eighth birthday, so we gave her one, and she pretended that it was her daughter. Now (at age ten) she doesn't play with it anymore and wants to give it to someone else.

When Ida was nine years old, she had six months of EMDR therapy combined with horse (equine) therapy. Her tantrums became less frequent but always occurred just after a therapy session and were still very intense. As the therapy progressed, the tantrums became less intense and eventually stopped towards the end of the therapy. She has tantrums now only sporadically, and they are not as violent as before.

She now also practices judo. We notice that it is good for her to do a sport where she makes physical contact with other children. She has found contact with the boys especially difficult, but she has become less fearful because she feels strong and confident.

At ten years of age, Ida has become joyful and relaxed. She can clearly and lovingly indicate if she does not like something. She still gets triggered occasionally by dishonesty, injustice, and disrespect for her boundaries, but these triggers don't cause tantrums any more. Often, it is enough that we acknowledge what she's feeling and listen to her express herself verbally. Then she relaxes again. She can stand up for herself and for others. She moves her body freely. We have a loving connection with her, and she has a clear need for physical closeness and touch that is safe and loving. We experience this as a very healthy sign of recovery. Her tantrums, crying, therapeutic play, and laughter in our loving presence have set her free. The following words describe how she is now: free, cheerful, creative, natural, social, and connecting.

Comments

Sexual abuse is a major trauma, and full recovery can take a long time. Children feel very confused and deeply betrayed by the secretive nature of the abuse and the fact that it usually occurs in the context of a loving or friendly relationship. During the months when it was occurring, Ida's behaviors indicated both hyperarousal (aggression, rudeness, and agitation) and dissociation (avoidance, withdrawal, and self-soothing activities such as moving her body back and forth while humming). She also suffered from bedwetting and nighttime fears, which are typical symptoms of sexual abuse.

Her healing began when she felt safe to talk with her parents about what had happened and when they believed her and supported her. She benefited from crying and raging, therapeutic play, laughter, and professional therapy. It was also helpful for her to talk to the police, share her experience with women who had been abused, ask questions, learn about sexuality and abuse, and practice judo.

Even after her parents knew what had happened, it was still difficult for Ida to volunteer information by telling a coherent narrative. Her mother had to learn the facts by asking specific questions that Ida could answer by saying yes or no. This apparent reluctance to talk about the trauma may have been caused by her feelings of shame. However, her inability to use language to describe the abuse was probably also due to the fact that traumatic memories are stored in a fragmented way in many different areas of the nervous system, which are unrelated to speech. For this reason, children (and even adults) find it difficult to put traumatic memories, emotions, and sensations into words.

Anger was one of Ida's major posttraumatic emotions. It can be challenging to cope with a traumatized child's violent hyperarousal behaviors (throwing things, kicking, and hitting) while trying to create emotional safety for healing to occur. Ida directed her aggression at her mother because she probably blamed her for allowing the boy to live with them and for not protecting her. Also, her mother was a handy target. However, violence and destructiveness are never part of the healing process. The mother needed to set loving, but firm, limits by intervening physically (without violence or punishment) to protect herself from being hurt. Ida was then able to release her angry emotions in a healthy way by crying and raging without attacking her mother. Her vigorous body movements while raging allowed her to do the self-defense actions that she was not able to do while the abuse was occurring. The mother wisely took care of her own emotional needs and processed her own anger separately in order to be emotionally available for her daughter's intense emotions.

Ida also benefited from therapeutic play. She laughed while pretending to send feces to her abuser and by burning drawings of him and his penis. She also laughed during power-reversal play with her mother who pretended to be a threatening, but incompetent, monster. Ida's need to take care of a doll representing a daughter of her own allowed her to create a feeling of protection which had been lacking during the abuse. All of these forms of play allowed her to revisit the trauma while feeling safe, and they empowered her and helped transform her memories.

Professional therapy further contributed to her recovery. Her tantrums at home immediately after her therapy sessions indicated that the therapy helped her revisit the trauma and activate the healing process.

With her parents' unwavering support, Ida has become a confident, joyful child who feels secure in her body and is able to trust and connect with other people in spite of her abuse. The experience will always be part of her life story, but her memory of it will be associated with a sense of mastery and successful recovery.

An eight-year-old boy recovers from a visit to the emergency room

A client brought her eight-year-old son for a play coaching session. This is my description of what took place in the session and what the mother continued to do at home.

Description of the case

At eight years of age, Lucas had a needle phobia (fear of injections) and expressed frequent anger at his mother after a traumatic medical incident. He had fallen off a couch at home and had cut his ear on the sharp edge of a coffee table. His mother supported his crying immediately after the accident. However, he sustained a later trauma in the hospital emergency room. His wound required surgical repair, and he was told that he would be given an injection to put him to sleep. Then, without any warning, two nurses suddenly appeared and gave him *two* injections, one in each thigh, and he screamed "no" before the sedation took effect. The experience left him feeling attacked, betrayed, and powerless.

I had a variety of toys available for him to use as he wished (including a pirate kit and a doctor kit), and he was immediately attracted to the pirate kit. He began with a power-reversal pillow fight with his mother in which he blindfolded her and also put toy handcuffs on her. She played her part by faking fright and falling dramatically to the floor.

Then I asked him if he would be willing to re-enact the hospital experience with his mother and me playing the roles of the nurses. He agreed and immediately armed himself with a plastic gun and a rubber pirate dagger! Pretending to be the two nurses, his mother and I each held a syringe from the doctor kit and playfully tried to sneak up on him so we could give the injections. He physically defended himself with the weapons while laughing, and we let him prevent us from touching his body. We repeated this activity several times, much to his delight.

Later, the mother continued power-reversal play at home. For example, she kept him laughing by pretending to be an incompetent nurse. She prepared water syringes outdoors and "accidentally" squirted them into the air while he successfully escaped. His anger eventually decreased, as did his needle phobia.

Comments

Anger at the mother (or primary parent) is a common posttraumatic symptom, even when the mother did not cause the trauma. Lucas probably felt betrayed by his mother in the emergency room because, from his point of view, she had failed to protect him from the unexpected and invasive double injections. The playful pillow fight helped him release some of that anger.

However, I felt that this play didn't address the underlying trauma, which was his inability to escape from the injections, so I suggested the play theme with the two nurses. This was another form of power-reversal play, because his mother and I pretended to be incompetent nurses who let our patient escape. His successful self-defense and escape from us helped him transform his memory of the trauma, and the laughter helped him release tension in his body and restore homeostasis.

This example is interesting in view of the fact that the original injury did not appear to cause lasting trauma, probably because his mother supported his crying immediately afterwards. Instead, the hospital experience traumatized him because he felt powerless and betrayed during a violation of physical boundaries (the injections). Furthermore, he had no opportunity to cry at the time, because the medication immediately sedated him.

Lucas went directly from a state of hyperarousal (screaming "no") into a state of deep sedation. Children are less likely to be traumatized by such interventions if medical personnel take the time to fully prepare them, obtain their consent, and reduce their level of terror before anesthetizing them. Unfortunately, this is not always possible, especially in emergencies.

A twelve-year-old girl recovers from an earthquake

I shared the following example about my daughter, Sarah, in my book, *Attachment Play*. I am including it here because it illustrates much of the information in this book.

Description of the case

When Sarah was twelve years old, we experienced an early-morning earthquake, which shook our house with several intense jolts but did not cause any damage. I ran into her room to reassure her. We stood under the door frame for safety, and she clung to me, trembling and crying. However, I feared the possibility of aftershocks and couldn't give her my full attention.

After the earthquake, she felt too terrified to sleep alone in her room, so I let her sleep with me. There was no improvement after a few weeks, so I started sleeping on a mattress in her room, with the goal of helping her adapt to her own bed. However, her fear did not subside, and she continued to feel too terrified to sleep alone in her room.

To help her revisit the trauma, I asked if she would be willing to play an earthquake game at bedtime, and she agreed to participate. (She felt very motivated to overcome her fear.) I sat on her bed in the dark for a few minutes of silence, then I suddenly yelled, "Earthquake!" while shaking her bed violently. She immediately started to laugh. We played this game for a few minutes every evening while I continued to sleep in her room.

Then one evening, after our usual earthquake game with much laughter, she said, "I'm scared." She wanted me to sit on her bed again, but I was already settled on my mattress, so I told her that she could come to me if she wanted to. However, she chose to stay in her own bed, where she cried hard for several minutes. Finally, she fell asleep. The following evening, she said to me, "You can sleep in your own room tonight. I'm not scared anymore." It had been exactly four weeks since the earthquake.

Comments

We cannot defend ourselves against an earthquake or run away from it. The only survival actions are to move away from windows or falling objects and stand under a door frame (or sturdy table) for safety. Just like evacuating by car from a wildfire, we are prevented from performing our instinctive reactions of fight or flight. Sarah's full-body trembling while crying in my arms during the earthquake helped her release some of the survival energy that had no other outlet because of her forced immobility. However, I was not very attentive to her emotional needs because of my own terror, so she could not complete her recovery at the time.

This example illustrates the concept of balance of attention. She felt too terrified to sleep alone in her room, but when I stayed with her, she felt so safe that there were no trauma triggers. I had to find a way to help her revisit the trauma while remaining with her. My playful re-enactment of earthquakes created the perfect balance of attention between fear and safety, which was necessary for her to begin healing.

When children become "stuck" with posttraumatic fears, play and laughter can help them release some of the tension and pre-pare them for deeper processing through crying. After playing and laughing during the earthquake game for a few days, Sarah was finally able to cry. Having been raised with this approach, she appeared to know instinctively that she needed to do so. In fact, she chose to remain in her own bed while crying, because she sensed that the slight distance from me created the necessary balance of attention.

Summary of Major Points

This book offers information about how trauma affects children and how parents can facilitate their recovery. Seven major themes summarize the information in it.

Awareness of childhood trauma is relatively new
The world has been slow to acknowledge childhood trauma, recognize its symptoms, and understand how to help children recover. Research in a variety of fields has led to our current understanding of childhood trauma.

Children are vulnerable
Children are vulnerable to trauma because of their immature brains, long period of dependency, and lack of information. Traumatic events can affect brain development and cause children to feel frightened, angry, sad, powerless, guilty, overwhelmed, and confused.

Trauma causes physiological reactions
During traumatic events, children use primitive survival mechanisms of hyperarousal and dissociation. These physiological states can help them cope temporarily by defending themselves, escaping, or becoming immobile and numb. If they don't have opportunities to heal, they will react strongly to later trauma triggers by resorting again to these same coping mechanisms. These physiological states can become chronic and maladaptive.

Children are born with the ability to recover from trauma
Children know instinctively how to heal from trauma, but they can do so only if certain conditions are met. When they feel emotionally safe and connected to a loving, supportive person, they can recover by revisiting the trauma and doing what their bodies need to do.

Healing from trauma is an active process
Recovery from trauma is an active process that differs from calming techniques. Children's biological healing mechanisms include laughter, specific kinds of play, crying, raging, and body movements.

Healing from trauma transforms children's memories
Children's memories change during the healing process. Their memory of the traumatic event becomes associated with feelings of power, confidence, and success instead of feelings of terror, rage, defeat, and powerlessness.

Children's posttraumatic symptoms and efforts to heal are often misunderstood
Children's posttraumatic symptoms and healing mechanisms are not always recognized for what they are. Instead, people misinterpret them as obnoxiousness, willful misbehavior, inborn character traits, immaturity, or psychiatric disorders. Many ineffective, and sometimes harmful, remedies have been used in the past and are still being used now.

Growing up with unhealed trauma can lead to later depression, anxiety, substance abuse, aggressive behavior, low self-esteem, poor interpersonal skills, inability to trust, and both physical and mental illness. It reduces people's ability to learn, think creatively, evaluate situations objectively, and make wise decisions. Additionally, it can cause people to focus exclusively on their own needs without taking other people into account.

The personal impact of unhealed trauma can, in turn, affect the entire world. Suppressed anger and terror may be significant contributing factors to violence and terrorism. In addition, leaders with unhealed childhood trauma establish economic, political, environmental, and national defense policies based on greed, faulty reasoning, personal insecurities, and irrational fears.

Even if you have no formal training as a therapist, you can play a major role in facilitating your children's recovery and contributing to a better, more peaceful world. In fact, you may be the person most qualified to help your children because you are their primary attachment figure, you interact with them on a daily basis, and you will immediately notice changes in their behavior and mood. Don't underestimate your importance, but be sure to ask for all the help and support you need.

Summary of major points

- Awareness of childhood trauma is relatively new.

- Children are vulnerable.

- Trauma causes physiological reactions.

- Children are born with the ability to recover from trauma.

- Healing from trauma is an active process.

- Healing from trauma transforms children's memories.

- Children's posttraumatic symptoms and efforts to heal are often misunderstood.

Definitions of Terms

Terms that are specific to Aware Parenting have an asterisk.

Attachment A term used by John Bowlby to refer to a child's bond with his or her mother. This term now also refers to attachment to the father and to anyone else who participates in caring for the child (called attachment figures).

* Attachment play Nine specific kinds of therapeutic interactive parent/child play described in the author's book, *Attachment Play*.

* Balance of attention A state in which a child feels emotionally safe while being reminded of a trauma. A balance of attention is necessary for emotional release and healing to occur (crying, play, laughter, etc.).

Behaviorism A field of psychology which focuses on observable and measurable changes in behavior caused by specific stimuli. One aspect of behaviorism, classical conditioning, is relevant for understanding conditioned fear responses and trauma triggers.

* Broken-cookie phenomenon A situation in which children cry apparently in response to a small incident, with the outburst seeming out of proportion to the event. The minor issue, such as the last cookie being broken, is used by the child as a pretext to release accumulated stress or tension resulting from a traumatic experience. (The broken cookie analogy was first used by Patty Wipfler.)

Classical conditioning An aspect of behaviorism which focuses on a form of learning first studied and described by Pavlov. It's a method of triggering involuntary autonomic reflexes (such as salivation) or emotional reactions (such as fear) in response to a previously neutral stimulus by pairing the neutral stimulus with one that causes the involuntary reflex or emotion. The previously neutral stimulus becomes a conditioned stimulus and the involuntary reaction or emotion becomes a conditioned response. Trauma triggers are classically conditioned stimuli, and posttraumatic fears are classically conditioned emotional responses. (Note: Classical conditioning is entirely different from operant conditioning, which is a form of learning based on the use of rewards and punishments following voluntary behaviors.)

Contingency play Playful interactive parent/child activities in which the adult's behavior is contingent on (or controlled by) the child's behavior, such as imitation games.

* Control patterns Repetitive or compulsive behaviors which are usually acquired during infancy and childhood to suppress crying and strong emotions. A typical control pattern is thumb sucking. Control patterns can put babies and children into states of mild dissociation. They are also called emotional suppression habits and self-soothing behaviors.

* Crying-in-arms approach The practice of holding babies while they cry (after all of their needs are met) and communicating love, empathy, and reassurance.

Developmental fears (also called normative fears) Fears that are typical of specific developmental stages and that are not caused by trauma.

Desensitization Decrease in reactivity to a trauma trigger. The approach to healing described in this book is a form of desensitization.

Developmental Trauma Disorder (DTD) A diagnostic term that was created by Bessel van der Kolk and rejected by the American Psychiatric Association.

Dissociation ("freeze or surrender") One of two primary physiological reactions to real or perceived threats. (The other is hyperarousal.) During dissociation, the parasympathetic nervous system is dominant, and children are quiet, passive, compliant, inattentive, unresponsive, and numb. Some children learn to dissociate with the help of a control pattern (such as thumb sucking) to suppress emotions.

Emotional release Any behavior that discharges tension from the nervous system and helps restore homeostasis. Forms of emotional release in children include crying, tantrums, trembling, laughter, certain kinds of therapeutic play, and body movements. These are also called healing mechanisms and tension-release mechanisms.

Emotional safety The feeling of being loved, connected, and fully protected from any kind of danger or harsh treatment.

Exposure therapy Any therapeutic approach that includes exposure to trauma triggers. Two kinds of exposure therapy are systematic desensitization and intense (or prolonged) exposure therapy. The approach described in this book involves gentle exposure to trauma triggers (revisiting trauma) and differs from these other two approaches.

Extinction The extinction of a classically conditioned fear response refers to its disappearance following exposures to fear-producing stimuli without the feared painful consequences.

Freud's seduction theory Freud's abandoned theory that the sexual abuse of young children was widespread and could lead to later psychological problems.

Homeostasis (or autonomic balance) A term originally created by Walter Cannon to refer to a physiologically balanced state of the body when it is not stressed. This term is used in this book to refer to the absence of both hyperarousal and dissociation when neither the sympathetic nor the parasympathetic nervous system predominates.

Hyperarousal ("fight or flight") One of two primary physiological reactions to real or perceived threats. (The other is dissociation.) During hyperarousal, the sympathetic nervous system is dominant, and children are agitated, distractible, impulsive, hypervigilant, defiant, reactive, aggressive, or destructive.

Intense (or prolonged) exposure therapy A form of exposure therapy based on the principle of extinction of a classically conditioned fear response in which traumatized people are repeatedly exposed to trauma triggers, which usually cause a strong emotional reaction.

* **Loving limit** A limit that is set lovingly, without punishment or rewards, which can give children a pretext to cry. A limit based on what a parent is willing (or not willing) to do can be an effective loving limit. (This term was created by Marion Rose, Ph.D.)

Memory reconsolidation The process by which the brain replaces memories with updated (modified) versions during retrieval.

Nondirective child-centered play An interactive parent/child activity in which adults provide a variety of materials (dolls, stuffed animals, blocks, toy vehicles, art materials, etc.) and let the child take the lead while they give their undivided attention.

Non-punitive discipline An approach to discipline that addresses children's underlying needs and feelings instead of using punishments or rewards.

* **Nonsense play** Playful interactive parent/child activities in which the parent or child purposely makes mistakes or engages in silly or exaggerated forms of behavior.

Parasympathetic nervous system Part of the autonomic nervous system which has multiple functions and plays a role in dissociation.

Post-Traumatic Stress Disorder (PTSD) A diagnostic term created by the American Psychiatric Association in 1980 in the third edition of their *Diagnostic and Statistical Manual of Mental Disorders (DSM-3)*.

Posttraumatic symptoms A variety of behaviors and emotions in children who are suffering from unhealed trauma.

* Power-reversal games Playful interactive parent/child activities in which the parent pretends to be weak, frightened, or incompetent (for example, a pillow fight in which the parent fakes weakness and falls to the floor).

* Regression play Playful interactive parent/child activities in which a child acts like an infant or younger child, and the parent responds by nurturing the child like an infant.

Re-traumatization An overwhelming feeling that the trauma is happening again. Children can become re-traumatized by being exposed to trauma triggers without feeling safe.

Revisiting trauma Being reminded of a trauma by exposure to a trauma trigger. Children sometimes choose to revisit trauma, typically through play. This is one of several conditions required for healing from trauma.

Sensations Perceptions through our senses. External sensations include sights, sounds, textures, temperature, pressure, odors, and tastes. Internal sensations include hunger, pain, nausea, dizziness, bladder or bowel fullness, body movement (kinesthetic and vestibular senses), and body position (proprioceptive sense), etc.

Sensitization Increase in reactivity to a trauma trigger. (See also desensitization.)

Separation games Playful interactive parent/child activities that incorporate separation and reunion between the parent and the child, such as peek-a-boo and hide and seek.

Shell shock A term used after World War I to refer to posttraumatic symptoms in combat veterans.

Stress Anything that disrupts physiological homeostasis. This engineering term was first used in a physiological sense by Hans Selye.

Symbolic play Any play that incorporates symbols. Therapeutic symbolic play helps children revisit trauma through toys or play themes which function as trauma triggers. Expressive symbolic activities such as drawing, modeling with clay, story-telling, or role-playing are also forms of symbolic play and can serve the same therapeutic function.

Sympathetic nervous system Part of the autonomic nervous system which has multiple functions and plays a role in hyperarousal.

Systematic desensitization An exposure therapy approach developed by Joseph Wolpe based on the principle of counterconditioning. The goal is to pair the conditioned fear-evoking stimulus (the trauma trigger) with an emotional state that is incompatible with anxiety, such as deep relaxation or pleasure.

Temper tantrum The healthy release of anger, frustration, and powerlessness through loud crying and active body movements. During a healthy tantrum, children are not violent or destructive.

Trauma (or traumatic event) Any event that causes physical or emotional pain or that a child perceives to be threatening (even if it's not). Traumatic events can range from a bee sting to major life-changing events such as the death of a parent. These events can lead to traumatization and posttraumatic symptoms.

Trauma trigger (also called trauma reminder) Anything that reminds a child of a traumatic event. Trauma triggers can be either external sensory impressions (such as sights, smells, or sounds) or internal sensory impressions (such as hunger, nausea, or body position). Trauma triggers that cause physiological or emotional reactions are classically conditioned stimuli. When children feel safe, trauma triggers can help them revisit trauma and activate natural healing mechanisms. When children don't feel safe, trauma triggers can cause re-traumatization.

Traumatic fears (also called posttraumatic fears or phobias) Fears that are caused by unhealed traumatic events and which differ from typical developmental fears. Traumatic fears are classically conditioned emotional responses.

Traumatic memory Memory of past personal traumatic experiences.

Traumatization A physiological and emotional condition involving an imbalance in the nervous system when a child has not yet healed after a traumatic event. Traumatized children are often in a state of hyperarousal or dissociation, especially when they are exposed to trauma triggers without feeling safe.

References

References for Chapter 1:
The Recognition of Childhood Trauma

Children are not miniature adults

Babenko, O. (2015). Stress-induced perinatal and transgenerational epigenetic programming of brain development and mental health. *Neuroscience and Biobehavioral Reviews*, 48, 70–91.

Coates, S. & Gaensbauer, T.J. (2009). Event trauma in early childhood: symptoms, assessment, intervention. *Child and Adolescent Psychiatry Clinics of North America*, 18(3), 611–626.

Thomason, M.E. & Marusak, H.A. (2017). Toward understanding the impact of trauma on the early developing human brain. *Neuroscience*, 342, 55–67.

Van der Kolk, B.A. (2003). The neurobiology of childhood trauma and abuse. *Child and Adolescent Psychiatric Clinics of North America*, 12, 293–317.

Wu, Y. *et al.* (2022). Association of elevated maternal psychological distress, altered fetal brain, and offspring cognitive and social-emotional outcomes at 18 months. *JAMA Network Open*, 5(4):e229244. doi:10.1001/jamanetworkopen.2022.9244.

Pioneers in childhood trauma

American Psychiatric Association (1980). *Diagnostic and Statistical Manual of Mental Disorders (DSM-3) (3rd edition)*.

American Psychiatric Association (2013). *Diagnostic and Statistical Manual of Mental Disorders (DSM-5) (5th edition)*.

Bowlby J (1999). *Attachment and Loss* (vol. 1), New York: Basic Books [originally published in 1969].

Cannon, W. (1932). *The Wisdom of the Body*. New York: W. W. Norton and Company.

Felitti, V.J. *et al.* (1998). Relationship of childhood abuse and household dysfunction to many of the leading causes of death in adults: the Adverse Childhood Experiences (ACE) study. *American Journal of Preventive Medicine*, 14 (4), 245–258.

Ferenczi, S. (1955). Confusion of tongues between adults and the child: the language of tenderness and passion. In S. Ferenczi, Ed. *Problems and Methods of Psychoanalysis*. London: Hogarth Press. [Paper presented at the 12th International Psycho-Analytic Congress in Wiesbaden, Germany in 1932.]

Fraiberg S. *et al.* (1975). Ghosts in the nursery. A psychoanalytic approach to the problems of impaired infant-mother relationships. *Journal of the American Academy of Child & Adolescent Psychiatry*, 14(3), 387–421.

Freud, S. (1896). The Aetiology of Hysteria. Paper presented to the Vienna Society for Psychiatry and Neurology.

Gaensbauer, T.J. (1995). Trauma in the preverbal period: symptoms, memories, and developmental impact. *Psychoanalytic Study of the Child*, 50, 122–149.

Kardiner, A. (1941). *The Traumatic Neuroses of War*. National Research Council. [Reprinted in 2012 by Martino Fine Books.]

Miller, A. (1990). *For your own Good: Hidden Cruelty in Child-Rearing and the Roots of Violence*. New York: Farrar, Straus and Giroux; 3rd edition. [Originally published in 1980 with the German title, *Am Anfang was Erziehung*.]

Pavlov I. (1927). *Conditioned reflexes: An investigation of the physiological activity of the cerebral cortex*. Oxford, England: Oxford University Press.

Perry, B.D., *et al.* (1995). Childhood trauma, the neurobiology of adaptation and 'use-dependent' development of the brain: how "states" become "traits." *Infant Mental Health Journal*, 16(4), 271–291.

Rank, O. (1924). *Das Trauma der Geburt*. Republished in 1998 by Psycho-sozial-Verlag, Germany. [English title: The Trauma of Birth.]

Selye, H. (1978). *The Stress of Life*. McGraw-Hill Education [first published in 1956].

Spitz, R.A. (1945). Hospitalism - An Inquiry into the Genesis of Psychiatric Conditions in Early Childhood. *Psychoanalytic Study of the Child*, 1, 53–74.

Terr, L. (1992). *Too Scared to Cry: Psychic Trauma in Childhood*. New York, NY: Basic Books.

Van der Kolk, B.A. (2014). *The Body Keeps the Score: Brain, Mind, and Body in the Healing of Trauma*. New York, NY: Penguin Books [reprinted in 2015].

Verny, T. & Kelly, J. (1981). *The Secret Life of the Unborn Child.* New York, NY: Dell Publishing.

Watson, J.B. & Rayner, R. (1920). Conditioned emotional reactions. *Journal of Experimental Psychology*, 3, 1–14.

Wolpe, J. (1954). Reciprocal inhibition as the main basis of psychotherapeutic effects. *Archives of Neurology and Psychiatry.* 72(2), 205–226.

Zero to Three: National Center for Infants, Toddlers and Families (1994). *Diagnostic Classification of Mental Health and Developmental Disorders of Infancy and Early Childhood.* Washington, DC: Zero to Three.

Human vulnerability to trauma

Haeusler, M. (2021). The obstetrical dilemma hypothesis: there's life in the old dog yet. *Biological Reviews*, 96(5), 2031–2057.

References for Chapter 2: The Neurobiology of Trauma

Hyperarousal and dissociation (during and after trauma)

Bryant, R.A. (2021). A critical review of mechanisms of adaptation to trauma: Implications for early interventions for posttraumatic stress disorder. *Clinical Psychology Review*, 85.

Carli, G. & Farabollini, F. (2022). Pain control in tonic immobility (TI) and other immobility models. *Progress in Brain Research*, 271(1), 253–303.

De Sousa, A. (2008). An open-label pilot study of naltrexone in childhood-onset trichotillomania. *Journal of Child and Adolescent Psychopharmacology*, 18(1), 30–33.

Fraiberg, S. (1982). Pathological defenses in infancy. *Psychoanalytic Quarterly*, LI.

Glover, E. (1942). Notes on the psychological effects of war conditions on the civilian population III. The "Blitz." *International Journal of Psychoanalysis*, 23, 17–37.

Janet, P. (1889). *L'automatisme psychologique.* Paris, France: Nouvelle Edition.

Klein, R.P. et al. (2009). Young children's responses to September 11th: The New York City experience. *Infant Mental Health Journal*, 30(1), 1–22.

Lanius, R.A. & Hopper, J.W. (2008). Reexperiencing hyperarousal and dissociative states in posttraumatic stress disorder. *Psychiatric Times* Vol. 25 No. 13.

Pavlov I. (1927). *Conditioned reflexes: An investigation of the physiological activity of the cerebral cortex.* Oxford, England: Oxford University Press.

Perry, B.D. et al. (1995). Childhood trauma, the neurobiology of adaptation and 'use-dependent' development of the brain: how "states" become "traits." *Infant Mental Health Journal*, 16(4), 271–291.

Perry, B.D. & Azad, I. (1999). Posttraumatic stress disorders in children and adolescents. *Current Opinion in Pediatrics*, 11, 310–316.

Putnam, F. W. (1989). Pierre Janet and modern views of dissociation. *Journal of Traumatic Stress*, 2(4), 413–429.

Roelofs, K. (2017). Freeze for action: neurobiological mechanisms in animal and human freezing. *Philosophical Transactions of the Royal Society B: Biological Sciences*, 372(1718),

Roth, A.S. *et al*. (1996). Naltrexone as a treatment for repetitive self-injurious behaviour: an open-label trial. *The Journal of Clinical Psychiatry*, 57(6), 233–237.

Schauer, M. & Elbert, T. (2010). Dissociation following traumatic stress. *Zeitschrift für Psychologie* (Journal of Psychology), 218(2), 109–127.

Solter, A. (2007). A case study of traumatic stress disorder in a 5-month-old infant following surgery. *Infant Mental Health Journal*, 28(1), 76–96.

Van der Kolk, B.A. (2000). Posttraumatic stress disorder and the nature of trauma. *Dialogues in Clinical Neuroscience*, 2(1), 7–22.

Van Huijstee, J. & Vermetten, E. (2018). The dissociative subtype of post-traumatic stress disorder: research update on clinical and neurobiological features. *Current Topics in Behavioral Neurosciences*, 38, 229–248.

Volchan, E. *et al*. (2017). Immobility reactions under threat: A contribution to human defensive cascade and PTSD. *Neuroscience and Behavioral Reviews*, 76(A), 29–38.

Trauma and memory

Bauer, P.J. (2002). Long-term recall memory: behavioral and neurodevelopmental changes in the first 2 years of life. *Current Directions in Psychological Science*, 11(4), 137–141.

Debiec, J., & LeDoux, J.E. (2006). Noradrenergic signaling in the amygdala contributes to the reconsolidation of fear memory: treatment implications for PTSD. *Annals of the New York Academy of Science*, 1071, 521–524.

Gaensbauer, T.J. (2002). Representations of trauma in infancy: Clinical and theoretical implications for the understanding of early memory. *Infant Mental Health Journal*, 23(3), 259–277.

Joseph, R. (1998). Traumatic amnesia, repression, and hippocampus injury due to emotional stress, corticosteroids and enkephalins. *Child Psychiatry and Human Development*, 29(2), 169–185.

Kida, S. (2019). Reconsolidation/destabilization, extinction and forgetting of fear memory as therapeutic targets for PTSD. *Psychopharmacology*, 236(1), 49–57.

Levine, P. (2015). *Trauma and Memory: Brain and Body in a Search for the Living Past.* Berkeley, CA: North Atlantic Books.

Peres J. *et al.* (2005). Psychological dynamics affecting traumatic memories: implications in psychotherapy. *Psychology and Psychotherapy*, 78(4), 431–47.

Perry, B.D. (1999). Memories of fear. In J Goodwin & R. Attias, *Splintered Reflections: Images of the Body in Trauma.* New York, NY: Basic Books.

Rosen, J.B. & Donley, M.P (2006). Animal studies of amygdala function in fear and uncertainty: relevance to human research. *Biological Psychology*, 73(1), 49–60.

Schwabe L, *et al.* (2014). Reconsolidation of human memory: brain mechanisms and clinical relevance. *Biological Psychiatry*, 76(4), 274–280.

Solter, A. (2008). A 2-year-old child's memory of hospitalization during early infancy. *Infant and Child Development*, 17, 593–605.

Terr, L. (1988). What happens to early memories of trauma? A study of twenty children under age five at the time of documented traumatic events. *Journal of the American Academy of Child and Adolescent Psychiatry*, 27, 96–104.

Van der Kolk, B.A. (2014). *The Body Keeps the Score: Brain, Mind, and Body in the Healing of Trauma.* New York, NY: Penguin Books [reprinted in 2015].

References for Chapter 3:
Posttraumatic Emotions and Basic Principles of Healing

Posttraumatic emotions

Terr, L. (1992). *Too Scared to Cry: Psychic Trauma in Childhood.* New York, NY: Basic Books.

Van der Kolk, B.A. (2000). Posttraumatic stress disorder and the nature of trauma. *Dialogues in Clinical Neuroscience*, 2(1), 7–22.

Van der Kolk, B.A. (2014). *The Body Keeps the Score: Brain, Mind, and Body in the Healing of Trauma.* New York, NY: Penguin Books [reprinted in 2015].

Basic principles of healing

Foa, E.B. & Kozak, M.J. (1986). Emotional processing of fear: Exposure to corrective information. *Psychological Bulletin*, 99 20–35.

Gaensbauer, T.J. & Siegel, C.H. (1995). Therapeutic approaches to posttraumatic stress disorder in infants and toddlers. *Infant Mental Health Journal*, 16(4), 292–305.

Hewey, J.H. *et al.* (2018). Comparing the effectiveness of EMDR and TF-CBT for children and adolescents: a meta-analysis. *Journal of Child and Adolescent Trauma*, 11(4), 457–472.

Levine, P.A. & Kline, M. (2008). *Trauma-Proofing Your Kids: A Parent's Guide for Instilling Confidence, Joy and Resilience*. Berkeley, CA: North Atlantic Books.

McLean, C.P *et al.* (2022). Exposure therapy for PTSD: A meta-analysis. *Clinical Psychology Review*, 91.

Oaklander, V. (2015). *Windows to Our Children: A Gestalt Therapy Approach to Children and Adolescents (2nd edition)*. Gouldsboro, ME: The Gestalt Journal Press.

Payne, P. *et al.* (2015). Somatic experiencing: using interoception and proprioception as core elements of trauma therapy. *Frontiers in Psychology*, 6, Article 93.

Reddy, L.A. *et al.* (2005). *Empirically Based Play Interventions for Children*. Washington DC: American Psychological Association.

Smith, N.B. *et al.* (2017). Fear extinction and memory reconsolidation as critical components in behavioral treatment for posttraumatic stress disorder and potential augmentation of these processes. *Neuroscience Letters*, 10(649), 170–175.

Creating emotional safety and connection

Miguez, G. *et al.* (2014). Classical conditioning and pain: Conditioned analgesia and hyperalgesia. *Acta Psychologica*, 145, 10–20.

Oaklander, V. (2015). *Windows to Our Children: A Gestalt Therapy Approach to Children and Adolescents (2nd edition)*. Gouldsboro, ME: The Gestalt Journal Press.

Uvnäs-Mobert, K. & Petersson, M. (2005). Oxytocin, a mediator of anti-stress, well-being, social interaction, growth and healing. *Zeitschrift für Psychosomatische Medizin und Psychotherapie*, 51(1), 57–80.

Van Puyvelde, *et al.* (2021). Why do we hunger for touch? The impact of daily gentle touch stimulation on maternal-infant physiological and behavioral regulation and resilience. *Infant Mental Health Journal*, 42, 823–838.

References for Chapter 4:
Natural Healing Mechanisms Part 1: Play and Laughter

Benefits of laughter

Bennett, M.P. & Lengacher, C. (2006). Humor and laughter may influence health: II. Complementary therapies and humor in a clinical population. *Evidence-Based Complementary and Alternative Medicine*, 3(2), 187–190.

Bennett, M.P. & Lengacher, C. (2008). Humor and laughter may influence health: III. Laughter and health outcomes. *Evidence-Based Complementary and Alternative Medicine*, 5(1), 37–40.

Fernandes, S.C. & Arriaga, P. (2010). The effects of clown intervention on worries and emotional responses in children undergoing surgery. *Journal of Health Psychology*, 13(3), 405–415.

Ventis, W.L. (1973). Case history: The use of laughter as an alternative response in systematic desensitization. *Behavior Therapy*, 4, 120–122.

Wilkins, J. & Eisenbraun, A.J. (2009). Humor theories and the physiological benefits of laughter. *Advances in Mind-Body Medicine*, 24(2), 8–12.

Yim, J. (2016). Therapeutic benefits of laughter in mental health: a theoretical review. *The Tohoku Journal of Experimental Medicine*, 239(3), 243–249.

Therapeutic play

Axline, V. (1981). *Play Therapy: The Groundbreaking Book That Has Become a Vital Tool in the Growth and Development of Children*. New York, NY: Ballantine Books.

Cohen, L. (2001). *Playful Parenting*. New York, NY: Ballantine Books.

Lin, Y.W. & Bratton, S.C. (2015). A meta-analytic review of child-centered play therapy approaches. *Journal of Counseling & Development*, 93(1), 45–58.

Oaklander, V. (2015). *Windows to Our Children: A Gestalt Therapy Approach to Children and Adolescents (2nd edition)*. Gouldsboro, ME: The Gestalt Journal Press.

O'Connor, K.J. et al. (2016). *Handbook of Play Therapy* (2nd Edition). John Wiley & Sons.

Reddy, L.A. et al. (2005). *Empirically Based Play Interventions for Children*. Washington DC: American Psychological Association.

Solter, A. (2013). *Attachment Play: How to Solve Children's Behavior Problems with Play, Laughter, and Connection*. Goleta, CA: Shining Star Press, 2013.

Stewart, A.L. et al. (2016). Neuroscience and the magic of play therapy. *International Journal of Play Therapy*, 25(1), 4–13.

Terr, L. (1983). Chowchilla revisited: the effects of psychic trauma four years after a school bus kidnapping. *American Journal of Psychiatry*, 140(12), 1543–1550.

References For Chapter 5:
Natural Healing Mechanisms Part 2: Crying And Raging

Spontaneous crying after trauma

deWeerth, C. & Buitelaar, J.K. (2007). Childbirth complications affect young infants' behavior. *European Child and Adolescent Psychiatry*, 16(6), 379–388.

Diego, M.A. (2005). Prepartum, postpartum, and chronic depression effects on neonatal behavior. *Infant Behavior and Development*, 28(2), 155–164.

Goodman, S.H. *et al.* (2011). Deconstructing antenatal depression: what is it that matters for neonatal behavioral functioning? *Infant Mental Health Journal*, 32(3), 339–361.

Klein, R.P. *et al.* (2009). Young children's responses to September 11th: The New York City experience. *Infant Mental Health Journal*, 30(1), 1–22.

Kotiniemi, L.H. (1997). Behavioural changes in children following day-case surgery: a 4-week follow-up of 551 children. *Anaesthesia*, 52, 970–976.

Nomura, Y. *et al.* (2019). Influence of in-utero exposure to maternal depression and natural disaster-related stress on infant temperament at 6 months: The children of Superstorm Sandy. *Infant Mental Health Journal*, 40(2), 204–216.

Sullivan, M.A. *et al.* (1991). Post-hurricane adjustment of preschoolers and their families. *Advances in Behavior Research and Therapy*, 13, 163–171.

Benefits of crying

Bergmann, T. (1965). *Children in the Hospital*. New York, NY: International University Press.

Bylsma, L.M. *et al.* (2019). The neurobiology of human crying. *Clinical Autonomic Research*, 29(1), 63–73.

Frey II, W.H. *et al.* (1981). Effect of stimulus on the chemical composition of human tears. *American Journal of Ophthalmology*, 92, 559–567.

Frey II, W.H. & Langseth, M. (1985). *Crying: The Mystery of Tears*. Minneapolis, MN: Winston Press.

Gracanin, A. *et al.* (2014). Is crying a self-soothing behavior? *Frontiers in Psychology*, 5(502), 1–15.

Gunnar, M. *et al.* (1992). The stressfulness of separation among nine-month-old infants: effects of social context variables and infant temperament. *Child Development*, 63, 290–303.

Gunnar, M. & Donzella, B. (2002). Social regulation of the cortisol levels in early human development. *Psychoneuroendocrinology*, 27(1–2), 199–220.

Karle, W. *et al.* (1973). Psychophysiological changes in abreaction therapy. Study 1: Primal Therapy. *Psychotherapy: Theory, Research and Practice*, 10, 117–122.

Kirsch, P. *et al.* (2005). Oxytocin modulates neural circuitry for social cognition and fear in humans. *The Journal of Neuroscience*, 25(49), 11489–11493.

Middlemiss, W. *et al.* (2012). Asynchrony of mother-infant hypothalamic-pituitary-adrenal axis activity following extinction of infant crying responses induced during the transition to sleep. *Early Human Development*, 88(4), 227–232.

Payne, P. *et al.* (2015). Somatic experiencing: using interoception and proprioception as core elements of trauma therapy. *Frontiers in Psychology*, 6, Article 93.

Solter, A. (1998). *Tears and Tantrums: What to Do when Babies and Children Cry*. Goleta, CA: Shining Star Press.

Uvnäs-Mobert, K. & Petersson, M. (2005). Oxytocin, a mediator of anti-stress, well-being, social interaction, growth and healing. *Zeitschrift für Psychosomatische Medizin und Psychotherapie*, 51(1), 57–80.

Vingerhoets, A. (1997). Crying, mood, and cortisol. *Psychosomatic Medicine*, 59, 92–93.

Vingerhoets, A. & Bylsma, L. (2007). Crying and health: Popular and scientific conceptions. *Psychological Topics*, 16(2), 275–296.

Viviani, D. *et al.* (2011). Oxytocin selectively gates fear responses through distinct outputs from the central amygdala. *Science*, 333, 104–107.

Woldenberg, L. *et al.* (1976). Psychophysiological changes in feeling therapy. *Psychological Reports*, 39, 1059–1062.

Misinterpretations of children's attempts to heal by crying and raging

Barr *et al.* (2018). Eight-year outcome of implementation of abusive head trauma prevention. *Child Abuse and Neglect*, 84, 106–114.

deMause, L. (1974). *The History of Childhood*. Lanham, MD: Roman and Littlefield Publishers, Inc.

Reijneveld, S.A. *et al.* (2004). Infant crying and abuse. *Lancet*, 364, 1340–1342.

Sulzer, J. (1748). *Versuch von der Erziehung und Unterweisung der Kinder* [An Essay on the Education and Instruction of Children], quoted in Alice Miller (1990), *For Your Own Good: Hidden Cruelty in Child-rearing and the Roots of Violence*. New York: Farrar, Straus and Giroux.

References for Chapter 6:
Additional Tips for Helping Children Recover

Developmental stages

Piaget, J. (1952). *The Origins of Intelligence in Children.* New York, NY: W. W. Norton & Co.

Piaget, J. (1952). *Play, Dreams and Imitation in Childhood.* New York, NY: W. W. Norton & Co.

Schaffer, H.R. & Emerson, P.E. (1964). The development of social attachments in infancy. *Monograph of the Society for Research in Child Development.* Vol. 29.

Trauma triggers and re-traumatization

Jordan, B. (2012). Therapeutic play within infant-parent psychotherapy and the treatment of infant feeding disorders. *Infant Mental Health Journal,* 33(3), 307–313.

Differences between calming techniques and healing techniques

Gunnar, M. *et al.* (1988). Adrenocortical activity and behavioral distress in human newborns. *Developmental Psychobiology,* 21(4), 297–310.

References for Chapters 7 and 8: Case Histories

Solter, A. (2007). A case study of traumatic stress disorder in a 5-month-old infant following surgery. *Infant Mental Health Journal,* 28(1), 76–96.

Solter, A. (2008). A 2-year-old child's memory of hospitalization during early infancy. *Infant and Child Development,* 17, 593–605.

About the Author

Aletha Solter, Ph.D., is a Swiss/American developmental psychologist, mother of two grown children, international speaker, workshop leader, and consultant. She studied with Dr. Jean Piaget at the University of Geneva, Switzerland, where she earned a Master's Degree in human biology. She holds a Ph.D. in psychology from the University of California, Santa Barbara. Her parenting books have been translated into many languages.

Dr. Solter has led workshops for parents and professionals in many countries and is recognized internationally as an expert on attachment, trauma, and non-punitive discipline. She founded the Aware Parenting Institute in 1990 in order to promote the philosophy of child rearing based on her work. There is a growing list of certified Aware Parenting instructors who are helping to spread this approach around the world.

She is available for lectures, workshops, and private consultations and can be reached at the address below.

The Aware Parenting Institute
P.O. Box 206
Goleta, CA 93116
U.S.A.

Phone & Fax: (805) 968–1868
e-mail: solter@awareparenting.com
website: www.awareparenting.com

What Is Aware Parenting?

AWARE PARENTING IS a philosophy of child rearing based on research in child development. It questions most traditional assumptions about children and proposes a new approach that can significantly improve relationships within a family. Parents who follow this approach raise children who are cooperative, compassionate, competent, nonviolent, and drug free. This philosophy is described in Dr. Aletha Solter's books.

For more information, please visit the Aware Parenting Institute website at www.awareparenting.com.

Aware Parenting consists of the following three elements:

Attachment-style parenting
- Natural childbirth and early bonding
- Plenty of physical contact
- Prolonged breast-feeding
- Prompt responsiveness to crying
- Sensitive attunement

Non-punitive discipline
- No punishments of any kind (including spanking, time-out, and artificial consequences)
- No rewards or bribes
- A search for underlying needs and feelings
- Anger management for parents
- Peaceful conflict resolution (family meetings, mediation, etc.)

Healing from stress and trauma
- Recognition of stress and trauma as primary causes of behavioral and emotional problems
- Emphasis on prevention of stress and trauma
- Recognition of the healing effects of play, laughter, and crying in the context of a loving parent–child relationship
- Respectful, empathic listening and acceptance of children's emotions